DAVID CARTER

with Brian Ward

IN MY MOTHER'S HOME

A True Story of a Young Boy's Life of Abuse

DEDICATION

There are many Police investigators and Children's Aid workers who continue to work tirelessly on behalf of children who endure neglect and abuse.

I applaud their tenacity and dedication.

A portion of the proceeds from the sale of this book will be donated to the Durham Children's Aid Foundation.

Foreword

In 1986, I was involved in a joint investigation between Durham Children's Aid Society, where I was the supervisor of the intake team, and Toronto Children's Aid Society investigating allegations of abuse involving a ten-year-old boy identified in this text as Nathaniel. It was during this time I met Detective Constable David Carter who was lead investigator from the Toronto Police Services. As part of a team, we unearthed a horrific story of abuse in the name of religion.

In my over three decades working as a front-line social worker, a supervisor and Child Victim Witness support worker, this case stands out as unique. Children's Aid societies in Ontario are governed by the Child and Family Services Act and are mandated to secure the safety and protection of children. We frequently collaborate with the police department whose focus is to investigate crime. Predictably, crime and child protection go hand in hand. In this particular story, Nathaniel was living with his parents in a home owned by the leader of what could only be identified as a Christian cult. The Pastor had a powerful influence and was instrumental in the cruel abuse of several children who had come into her church.

Sadly, the incidence of child abuse is well-known in our culture and has even become the fodder of entertainment. I wonder if we are becoming inured to this terrible reality. As a news report or a court record, these stories are easy to ignore, but IN MY MOTHER'S HOME gives a voice to a ten-year-old who didn't have that opportunity as a child. It puts a name and a face to abuse that makes it poignant and too difficult to ignore. There is nothing objective or coolly scientific about this story. It is written from the heart, and the gut-wrenching truth of Nathaniel's story is palpable. The victims of abuse often don't have the context of normal - removed from mainstream society, denied schooling - they don't know that what they experience is not typical. Worse, they often interpret the abuse as a consequence of their own wickedness. If caught, the perpetrators are punished for a period of time, but the victims carry the scars for a lifetime.

Although Nathaniel's circumstances were unusual, the reality of the abuse is not. This book invites the reader to question appearances, to recognize the need to respond and to acknowledge the challenging work of police and social service workers who are dedicated to the protection of children.

Lynn Factor C.M., O. Ont, MSW, RSW, LL.D

Preface

It was a warm summer evening, about 6:00pm, on July 9, 1986, when my police search warrant team rolled down a Pickering driveway in a dusty procession of two unmarked police cars and one marked police car. The team consisted of myself, several Detectives from the Durham Regional Police Service, a Children's Aid Society worker from Durham Region and a uniformed officer from one of the Metropolitan Toronto Police Force's* downtown divisions. His presence seemed to be out of place but became significant as we progressed.

The air was heavy and smelled of dry hay. Heat bugs welcomed our arrival with a chorus of chirps and buzzes.

It had been one month to the day that I became immersed in the world of religious cults, and it was an investigation that would stay with me forever.

We were preparing to enter a century old stone house that we had come to know as the scene of horrendous child abuse and torture under the guise of a religious cult.

The purpose of the raid was to search the house for evidence of any criminal acts and enforce a Warrant of Apprehension for an abused child who we believed to be in one of two homes.

I had set up two teams of officers and Children's Aid Society workers. The plan was to strike at the two locations simultaneously.

My team was to search the farmhouse in Pickering which

was the reported headquarters of a religious cult which, at that time, went by the name of His Rest Christian Fellowship.

Pickering, in the 1980's, was a small city just east of Toronto, Ontario and was just starting to see the urban sprawl that would eventually swallow it up. Small family farms still clung to the landscape.

The team was tense with anticipation. I was after the prize. The big catch. A female Pastor who ruled with an iron fist.

As we approached the house, we saw two young boys tending a vegetable garden. They appeared like characters from a previous era; tiny, fragile, and scruffy. Like characters out of a Dickens novel.

The boys stopped their work and stared as one of the officers got out of the car and approached them.

"Are you Nathaniel?" the officer asked a boy.

The boy nodded.

"I am Detective Sturgeon from Durham Regional Police, and this is Lynn Factor, a case worker with the Durham Children's Aid Society. Would you come with us?"

Without a word, he dropped the hoe he was carrying and got into the back seat of the car.

His life of abuse and beatings was now over. His tortured life forms part of the story of abuse and neglect while under the care of his own parents and a self-proclaimed Pastor.

The names of the suspects and the victims have been changed but the identities of the Investigators, Children's Aid workers, Crown Attorneys, and Judiciary are real.*The name of the Metropolitan Toronto Police Force was officially changed to the Toronto Police Service in 1998

Acknowledgement

There are many people that I would like to thank for their input and assistance in helping to make this book a reality.

It would be impossible to begin thanking all the people involved in this investigation without first thanking "Ricky".

Before Ricky was brave enough to report his abuse, he spent almost eight years living with, and carrying, this burden on his mind constantly.

The very thought of airing your dirty laundry in public is beyond most people's comprehension, let alone when it involves years of abuse.

Abuse cases, especially 'historic' ones are mostly reported years, or decades, after the abuse has taken place. Coming forward is one of the most difficult steps a victim of abuse takes after having to carry around these heavy memories on their shoulders, sometimes for their entire life.

It was Ricky's selfless disclosure in order to help his little friend, "Nathaniel", that drove him to come forward.

Robert Parsons, the Social Worker with the Board of Education for the City of Scarborough, who got the ball rolling by calling the Toronto Children's Aid Society. His assistance and support were invaluable in helping Ricky report his abuse.

Jim Langstaff, the Toronto Children's Aid Society case worker, who contacted me for assistance to commence a joint investigation and assist with Ricky's interview. I believe that his ability to bond with Ricky set the groundwork to enable a full criminal investigation. Jim is retired now yet still puts his skills to use assisting the Durham Children's Aid Society.

Lynn Factor, at the time of our investigation, was the case worker with the Durham Children's Aid Society and was assigned to assist with my investigation as well as Nathaniel's well being.

Lynn spent countless hours with me listening to the tape recordings of our interviews with Nathaniel, trying to get down an accurate written account from his audiotaped statement. This was a difficult and time-consuming process, as so often the victim lowers their voice and background noise makes it difficult to decipher their words.

Lynn has continued to dedicate her life to helping children. In January 2018, Lynn was named a Member of the Order of Canada "for her contributions to the field of social work and for her dedication to improving the lives of our most vulnerable children."

Ricky's brother, "Ron", was an immense support to Ricky and helped him to understand that by becoming a witness at a trial, that he was not the one in trouble. Again, Ricky's sheltered past had him thinking that he would be in trouble if he testified.

Ron also provided a wealth of information that helped to seal up any gaps in the investigation. This included airing the dirty laundry of his childhood. Certainly not an easy feat to accomplish. Ron is retired now and enjoys the northern life outdoors in his kayak.

Linda, my Investigative Office clerk, for her dedication and professional manner.She was tasked with listening to, and transcribing, many hours of taped interviews. Some of the information was not easy to listen to.

Durham Regional Police Detectives Sturgeon and McKechnie for all their help with locating the Pastor's home in Durham and with the execution of the search warrant. They also brought a sense of humour, saying that I was the anti-Christ taking down the cult empire.

As an investigator, a sense of humour always helps the mind to avoid keeping tragic events like this from being locked up inside.

All the officers and staff at 42 Division who assisted in some way to help this investigation get to the courts and culminate with the first successful conviction of its kind in Canada.

The Crown Prosecutors Ms. Karen Dunlop and Mr. John McMahon (now Justice McMahon) for their tireless dedication and knowledge in taking these criminal matters through the court system with successful results.

Nathaniel's wife, who helped fill in the parts of Nathaniel's life after the abuse, while still grieving the loss of her husband and father of her son. I truly believe that with her, Nathaniel was the happiest he had ever been in his life.

Nathaniel's friend from grade school who was like his sister and became a person of stability in his life. I appreciate her courage and insight and admire the friendship she built, and maintained, with Nathaniel.

Brian Ward who gave me the push to start putting pen to paper in 2019 and wrote the foundation of the book. His insights and experience were invaluable.

Marilyn White for her beta editing and completing all the finishing touches to the book.

Carolyn Buyers for her initial hand drawn rendering of the Scarborough stone house as it appeared during the 1986 investigation.

Natalie Adams for her artistic talent and hand drawn reproduction of Carolyn's Scarborough stone house adding in the "Boy in the window" and the kitchen add on. It is a perfect representation of how the house would have looked during the time of the Pastor's reign.

TABLE OF CONTENTS

1

Chapter 1

MY POLICING CAREER

Why in the world would anyone in their right mind want to become a police officer? This question continues to pop up in my mind even to this day.

In December 1977 I was sworn in, and then commenced a three-month training program both here in Toronto and at the dreaded Ontario Police College in Aylmer, Ontario

Why dreaded?

Recruits were separated from their families, functioned with regimented behaviours in class, and practiced endless marching drills on the parade square. Recruits studied incessantly instead of enjoying themselves like other 20 year olds. Boot polishing, pressing our uniforms, making sure our hair was cut to regulation and making sure we did not get yelled at by the drill sergeant were all part of our day.

Drill sergeants were a peculiar breed of police officer. They were chosen for their loud voices, their ability to make a recruit feel like a child, and their incredibly well-polished boots.

Weren't we police officers instead of soldiers being trained to head into battle? I soon found out that I too was heading for a career that had its share of battles. Some people hated the police while others just felt uncomfortable in our presence. What other career provided the excitement, stresses, and pressures that I would soon encounter on the streets of Toronto?

I was proud of the uniform, proud to be a cop and proud that I would be serving and protecting my community. Graduation day was one of the best moments of my life. I would be patrolling in uniform, arresting criminals, and living a life of adventure that few could say they would ever experience.

When I returned to the city, I spent a short period of time at the Toronto Police College. One day my instructor asked the class who had a licence to operate a motorcycle. My hand flew up in anticipation of cruising the streets on a brand-new shiny Honda motorcycle with flashing red lights.

And so, I found myself, in September 1978, assigned to a downtown traffic unit and living the dream. I wore shiny leather leggings as part of the uniform, and I looked like a million bucks.

Bad guys were cautious, and women swooned as I patrolled the streets; or at least that was what I imagined.

Summer turned into fall and soon winter would be approaching. No problem, I thought, as the police issued warm jackets and leather gauntlets would keep the cold at bay. The windshield of my bike cut the wind and my patrolling continued even during the first light snowfall.

Soon the days grew shorter, and the temperatures dipped to the point where it became uncomfortable to ride for an entire shift. The Toronto Police Service had a long history of operating their motorcycles during the winter and we shifted from the

Hondas to the old dependable Harley Davidson motorcycles with a sidecar for balance on the winter roads.

Some motorcycle officers wore several layers of long underwear, sweaters, and anything else for insulation that kept the cold at bay. I even heard of some wearing nylons. Rumour had it that some had and begun putting magazines into their long underwear at their knees to stop them from freezing. It became painful to dismount from my bike because my joints just did not like to be frozen.

The cold became too much for me and I applied for a transfer out of the traffic unit and into a police unit that sent officers on patrol in nice warm cars. This was a great idea in theory, but my Inspector did not want to let me go, so a transfer became very difficult.

I reverted to Plan B, working diligently at enforcement, and occasionally offering my supervisors boxes of donuts. I finally got my transfer, thanks to an understanding Staff Sergeant who was filling in for the Inspector.

The Toronto Police Service covered a vast area and was divided into five geographical districts. These districts were in turn divided into smaller numbered units called divisions. I had set my sights on going to 42 Division which covered the northeast section of the city.

During the late 1970's and early 1980's, 42 Division consisted of smaller housing projects, low- rise industrial units, a large railway yard, the Toronto Zoo, and farmland. I was happy to learn what policing was all about.

Midnight shift was boring and sometimes the most excitement I had was rounding up stray horses from Lionel's Pony Farm. However, I learned by keeping my eyes open. I was good at spotting criminals and my arrest rate began to climb.

Geared to low-income townhouses and high-rise residential complexes that dotted the division and took up a lot of our time handling everything from domestic quarrels to assaults and even the occasional murder.

Around this time, policing theories began to change, and a decision was made to move some officers from their cars to walking a beat within some of these communities. I was interested in a divisional unit called the Area Foot Patrol. By 1984 I found myself out of a car and onto the streets, walking a beat.

My foot patrol partner, Constable Dave McManus, and I soon became a force to be reckoned with among the youth of these communities, but we treated them decently. We learned that one of them had spray painted our names on a wall in one of the buildings. We learned it was their way of showing respect, and maybe some fear.

About a year later, I wanted to move into another area of policing and was selected to transfer into the division's Youth Bureau where trained Investigators dealt exclusively with young offenders under 18 years of age.

The Criminal Code of Canada has always made a distinction between adult and youth criminals. Our office operated like a Detective Office except our clients were younger and we were able to resolve a lot of offences through mediation and by working closely with parents, the local Children's Aid Society, and the schools. Although youths still committed crimes, they were not to be tried in adult court and were dealt with by special prosecutors, judges, and support staff.

Sadly, investigating child abuse was part of our mandate, as were sexual assault investigations involving children.

Most of our work was done within elementary schools and

we were usually accompanied by trained Children's Aid Society workers. The teamwork approach really paid off for us, our reputation grew, and my partner and I were often called in by a school or Children's Aid worker.

One case involved an 11-year-old boy who had been engaging in sexual touching of little girls whenever he wanted. This was brought to our attention when one of the victim's mothers learned what had happened and called the police.

It is important to remember that the suspect was under 12, which is under the age of criminality, and other than a stern talking to, there was nothing we could do.

A short time later that day, we were called to another home where our suspect had inappropriately touched a three-year-old girl who was still in diapers. As he had just celebrated his 12th birthday, we arrested him on the spot.

Our witness was allowed to testify despite her age and the boy was convicted. I received a Letter of Commendation from the Prosecuting Assistant Crown Attorney for my work with the three-year-old.

Another case involved a young child and an alleged sexual assault. This investigation took a startling twist once we became involved. We received information from uniformed officers that a three-year-old girl had been allegedly sexually assaulted. The prime suspect was her 16-year-old uncle. Uniformed officers began the investigation and learned from the girl's grandmother that her father was on his way with a shotgun to take care of our suspect. The young girl had told her grandmother, and the officers, her pubic area was sore, and her throat hurt as well, pointing to her chin.

Through investigation, I learned that her sore pubic area was the result of a jump up onto a kitchen bench. And her sore throat?This injury had occurred when her uncle, while helping her zip up her winter jacket, pinched her chin in the zipper.Case solved.

It may seem strange to some that this type of work didn't outwardly bother me but internally, I chose not to take my work home and built up a "Blue Wall" with those around me.

I experienced nightmares where I was involved in a high-risk police event, and I drew my gun to protect myself. In the nightmare it was a stapler in my hand instead of my gun. It would never fire. Maybe I had been working in an office far too long! But I loved the work, and we did a lot of good for the community.

I stayed in the Youth Bureau for the next six months and found myself transferred to the divisional Detective Office for more than a year. A vacancy opened in the Youth Bureau, and I made the move back, where I remained for another year or so.

My official rank was Detective Constable, but a promotional process was upcoming, and I was eager to take part. The next rank in the policing structure was Sergeant.This was a uniform supervisory position, and its investigative equivalent was Detective. I studied hard, had a good interview for the position and was successfully promoted to Sergeant. I was transferred to 41 Division which is the main police division in Scarborough. After a short six-month probationary period, I transferred to the Criminal Investigative Bureau Office as a Detective.

After more than a decade in that role, I wanted a change of pace and transferred to 31 Division which is located in the north central area of Toronto. I remained in this division until my retirement in 2008.

It is ironic that shortly after my retirement I had the recurring nightmare about a high-risk take down. However, this time, I had my gun in my hand instead of a stapler. When I pulled the trigger, it fired but only at an invisible target.

In the early summer of 1986, during my first deployment in 42 Division's Youth Bureau, I became involved in the investigation of a small religious cult in our area.

This investigation led to the first successful Canadian prosecution of crimes committed by cult members against other cult members, including children.

This investigation is the reason that I finally wanted to share my story and you will quickly understand why it haunted me.

2

Chapter 2

RELIGIOUS CULTS

In November 1978, the world was horrified to learn about the mass suicide in Guyana, of 900 followers of a religious cult leader named Jim Jones, who had decided to remove his cult members from the face of the earth. They blindly followed his orders and drank fruit juice that was laced with poison. It became known as the "Jonestown Massacre".

With the ensuing publicity, other cults soon gained notoriety around the world and to this day continue to hold their followers in an iron grip.

Cults such as the Japanese Aum Sect, China based Falun Gong, and numerous other sects around the world practising polygamy have raised the specter of mind control.

But what are they and how do they operate?

It is important to understand the psychology of cults, how they operate, and the effects they have on their followers.

"A cult is an unorthodox, deviant religious group that is devoted to a person, thing, or set of ideas. People who join cults are often dissatisfied with the world or unsure of their place in it. Cults offer answers, asserting that the world is corrupt and unreliable. It can be difficult to leave a cult. The world outside can seem frightening and evil.

Cults usually teach their followers how to behave, live, and think, and sometimes how to use their money, what to wear, and where to live. Most cults require worship of, or dependence upon, the leader and encourage dependence upon other members or the whole group. Some demand a promise of commitment, an initiation ceremony, financial input, active evangelism, and/or participation in ritual.

Attributes include.

A strong leader

Revelations/apocalyptic vision

Good works

Use of scripture from an established religion.

New or revised doctrine

Control and rules

Indoctrination

Isolation

Close relationships

False teaching/prophecy"

Source: https://omf.org/ca/

The quote comes with permission from a Canadian-based religious group which is an arm of the Overseas Missionary Fellowship which began in early 20th century China. It has spread around the world with its focus on helping Asian countries in preserving Christianity during ever- changing conflicts.

My career took a turn when I was called upon to investigate and prosecute a small religious cult that had emerged in our division as well as in the adjacent Durham Region. I was a Youth Bureau investigator who was accustomed to dealing with young criminals. I was not prepared to do battle with religion.

I reached out to our Intelligence Unit and other police services for any assistance in dealing with cults, however no one had ever been involved in any investigations with cults. I found myself on my own researching, learning, and trying to understand what I was dealing with.

Toronto resident, Ian Haworth, became one of my main sources for information on cults. He continues to be regularly consulted by the media and provides help to those seeking to remove themselves from the cult lifestyle.

Ian had read a Toronto Police Service Press Release about my investigation, and he reached out to offer assistance. He provided us with an intimate understanding of how cults work including his own experience from his involvement in a cult.

This is his story, and it reveals how easy it was for him to be lured into the cult lifestyle and how difficult it was for him to leave.

During a telephone interview for this book, Mr. Haworth advised that had immigrated to Canada from England in 1972. He recounted how he became involved in a cult when he was employed by a Toronto based telecommunications company.

He explained that there are two different types of cults: one dealing with religion and the other dealing with lifestyle changes. His is the story of a lifestyle cult but he pointed out that both types of cults are insidious and can ensnare almost anyone.

"In 1978, I was walking in downtown Toronto when I met a good- looking young woman on the street. She struck up a conversation and asked me if I wanted to improve my lifestyle and told me it was time to give back to my community.

Good idea I thought, and she invited me to a meeting later that week at a large downtown hotel.

It was run by a group called PSI Mind Development and it turns out they had been given tax free status as a charity by the government.

I went along to check it out. I was soon bored almost to tears, so I went out into a hallway for a smoke. Someone stopped to chat with me and asked if I wanted to stop my serious smoking habit. Why not I asked myself? So, it was off to another meeting.

Cults have two main purposes; to change lifestyles or take up a religion and I became involved in changing my lifestyle to stop smoking. Little did I know that the group would soon take me into a lifestyle that I could not change on my own.

It was nothing but constant meetings where they demanded all my money to support the cause and took control over my mind to the point where I wanted to quit my job and get fully involved. In fact, I drafted a letter of resignation which my boss wisely filed in her desk drawer instead of acting on it. I had lost the ability to think on my own and became someone else.

I later found out that the upwardly mobile are the easiest for a cult to achieve total control. And the techniques they used on me are like ones used to this day to recruit terrorist candidates. Within a few days, I was totally under control of the cult, and I was trying to recruit my friends.

The disturbing aspect is that it is not illegal to establish total mind control over someone and force them into turning over their money to finance the cult and its leaders.

My friends became alarmed by my drastic change and one of them gave me an article that was just published in the Toronto Star by reporter Sydney Katz. It was a full feature on PSI Mind

Development and how they are a mind control cult.

I read it, the light bulb went on, I got scared, and I fell apart at the seams. I panicked and called the second in command of PSI who told me to go away and made some anti-Semitic remarks about Katz.

I didn't know where to turn so I called Katz who immediately offered to help and put me in touch with a CBC producer Peter Scott who was a main source for Katz' story. With his help, I began my journey to escape the cult after only two and a half weeks.

It took me 11 months to fully recover, and I learned my symptoms included signs of Post-Traumatic Stress Disorder. But it also steeled me to begin a new career dedicated to helping cult victims and exposing the totality of mind control. I founded the Council of Mind Abuse with Peter Scott."

Together they worked to educate about cults and helped to remove those involved. Haworth's work continued in Toronto until 1986 at which point, he moved back to England. He continued his work with the charity "Cult Information Centre" where he remains to this day.

3

Chapter 3

THE HORROR UNFOLDS: RICKY SPEAKS

It was June 9th, 1986 and my partner Detective Constable McManus and I were in the Youth Bureau office when the phone rang. I picked up the receiver and found myself speaking with Jim Langstaff, a worker with the Toronto Children's Aid Society. He requested I meet with him at Sir Wilfred Laurier High School to speak with a 19-year-old student. Langstaff assured me that this student's story would be of great interest.

Later that afternoon we met with a school counsellor, and the student, who we will name Ricky. Over a period of two years, Ricky had been counselled at the high school for behavioural problems. It wasn't until the day we all met, that the story of Ricky's torment in his mother's church finally spilled out.

The initial interview lasted two hours. As was my standard practice, this interview, along with Ricky's subsequent interview, was tape recorded.

The information we learned from these interviews was astounding.

Ricky was one of three children being raised in a church environment that became more bizarre as the children grew older.

When Ricky turned 17, he escaped his mother's home and went to live with his father. His fear during the interview, however, was for the welfare of a young boy, Nathaniel, who was still living in the house.

Langstaff began the questioning.

"Perhaps we could get some understanding of when the church started. Do you recall that?", he asked.

"Well, I was pretty young then. That was about nine or ten years ago. That was when my dad was still with my mother and that didn't seem to work out because of the church 'because she was spending too much time with them'. It became her obsession, so my father left".

There were three boys in the family although the eldest, Jeremy, had left earlier to become an overseas missionary.

"So that's basically when it started and a few years later, my brother left to live with my dad. I stayed with my mother".

Langstaff asked who was part of the church at that time.

"Well, there's me and my mother and then a whole group of other people. Some that are still with them, and others have left. Then we moved to another location. And more people came to live there until finally there was, like, ten people besides me and my mother".

Langstaff asked how many children were in the house.

"Ah, well, Nathaniel was with us basically from the beginning, like I've known him since he was just a few months old. And, ah, he wasn't always living there. He was with his mother and father, and they were divorced. So, Nathaniel stayed with his father and then he moved in with his father to my mother's house."

When asked how many adults were in the home, Ricky said many of them were teenagers.

"Basically, all dealt with drug problems and, ah, you know, weak minded people."

"Why would they come to this church?", Langstaff asked.

"Well, they wouldn't really they were sort of duped into coming. Like they found a place and my mom would offer them a place to crash and then she gradually started to get her tentacles over them.

My mother, uh by referral like other people, some other people would tell them about the boarding house, whatever, and she would pick up hitch hikers and take them. She liked to do that. Some of them were old school friends of my eldest brother.

It was basically they all had one thing in common, that they were all basically weak minded and like a Pastor, my mother offered a safe haven for them, and it would appear like a unit. It would, well it was part of like everything they did.

It was supposed to be Christian, right. Their life was directed towards that and towards her ministry and the furtherance of her church which was God's will in her word. Any other was outside of the church was evil by the way of Satan and the world. So, like you became, if you left, you felt really guilty and couldn't handle and being weak minded people, they wouldn't leave.

And all that, she affected all of their decisions and whatever they made towards, like partners or whatever. So, it was pretty gradual until they couldn't really depend on anyone else but her, and she had them in her grasp that saw snatches here and there. I saw the way the other people lived and that got me to thinking but I didn't really see what was going on."

Ricky told us that he had gone to school until he was 11 or 12 years old and had finished grade six.

"And those years, grade four, five and six I had some problems in school with schoolwork. My mother wouldn't let me read certain readers because they were evil, and I wasn't allowed to take books out of the library.

I had to bring my Bible to school and read it and preach to my classmates, be a shining light for Jesus and all this stuff."

At the age of 11, Ricky was taken out of school and began to be home schooled. Unlike other boys his age, he was forced to stay in the house, reading his Bible and attending a few of the programs his mother taught.

Harsh discipline for Ricky was common in the home and, once his description unfolded, we all shuddered. It was at this point in the interview that the horrible details of the abuse came to light.

Ricky talked about it as if was just a normal course of action in his life at home.

I let Langstaff conduct most of the interview with Ricky because he was comfortable with him, and the information flowed smoothly. Ricky was a strapping young man who reminded me of a farmer's son.

Langstaff asked him what kind of discipline his mother gave out.

"Yeah, interpretation of the Bible she was like a tyrant. Basically, what she had to say was directly from God and I couldn't question her and if I ever made the mistake of doing it, which I sometimes did, then I was severely punished for it".

"Sometimes I had no food or sent to my room or beatings, or I would have to confess in front of everyone on my knees".

"Sometimes she would take a stick or sometimes she would take a large piece of wood, like a two by four, stuff like that, across the back and rear end. That was basically it and if I cried, then I got more. That's the same that happened to Nathaniel. And that happened a lot".

"Usually, my mother had a large stick that she kept for the purpose or at the time what was at hand. You know like a wooden coat hanger of a large stick or large pieces of wood. If I didn't cry, if I stood there, then that infuriated my mother again because she wasn't getting, she was not breaking me. My will never broke. They stopped because she was tired. She couldn't beat me anymore because they went on, usually for a long time".

"And then she would stop and preach to me and then start again and stuff like that. I was standing and she made me bend over, all the time she would be preaching and reciting. I'd have to say a prayer for God's forgiveness and saying that over and over again."

About the time the beatings began, Ricky's mother became closely acquainted with a cult member named Doug. He became an integral part of the abuse.

"It wasn't really the beatings that I was afraid of because after a while you accept them. I thought that was the way it went. That everyone got spanked when they were a kid, but I realize now that there is a difference between spanking and beating and discipline and you know, torture and discipline. I was more afraid of, like being locked in my room or locked in a closet or things like that.

"Nothing I could do would help either; whatever I tried wouldn't work".

"I tried crying. I would say I was sorry. I would say I'm sorry mom, is there anything I could do. I'd do whatever I could. I would tell her that I was going to pray and ask God to forgive and do whatever I had to escape discipline".

"It usually didn't work. Usually, it was something set in her mind. She would at times praise me as being her little Ricky, her little Chosen One and at other times I was evil. Then I would have to confess in front of all the people there, in front of her little church. I would have to kneel in the center of the circle and confess to anything that I had done wrong and a lot of things that I hadn't done wrong".

"I was disciplined for questioning her authority, well questioning her interpretation of the Bible. I recall I was sent to my room for two days for wearing a pair of jeans.

At this point Ricky described how he was given only clothes his mother bought at a second-hand store and he was embarrassed to wear them.

"It was part of her whole set up. I wouldn't want to go out in society because of the way I was dressed and the way I looked. Um, so I had no desire to go out because I looked ridiculous. I had no pride, and which was part of her whole set up. But when I wore those jeans, I was disciplined for it."

Ricky was asked how would the beatings stop.

"Usually, she was tired. She couldn't beat me anymore cuz they went on usually for quite a long time.It was basically … . Like if I went against her… I was going against God and whatever she wanted me to do, and I did it because now I am going to Hell and I'm going to be burned."

He was asked, "Minutes or like 10 minutes?"

"Oh, longer than that" "And then she would stop and preach to me and then start again."

He was asked, "Would you have to sit still, or would you be standing or laying down?

"I was standing usually. She made me bend over."

He was asked, "Would she ask you to take your clothes off?"

"She usually told me to take my pants down or take my shirt off."

He was asked if she preached to him during the beatings.

"Sometimes. It was something she would say, and I would have to say a prayer for God's forgiveness and keep saying that over."

"I guess she was realizing that I was growing up a bit too fast for my britches and that I might start to question her methods. Other times I felt rage and I guess she saw that.I don't know what stopped me but then I would have…. destroyed her in my own way."

Langstaff was concerned about any injuries Ricky suffered and if he ever got any medical attention.

"I think I might have, my spine, eh, is crooked and I get back pains a lot. I had bruises, bruises and that."

Ricky told us he couldn't continue talking about his own abuse and switched to speaking about Nathaniel, a little boy who was still living at home in Scarborough with his parents, Susan, and Greg.

"Nathaniel wasn't learning to walk when you would expect it. He wasn't gaining strength. When he was younger, I guess he was about a year and a half, whenever kids are supposed to start learning to walk and he was in the situation that he wasn't talking very well, and he was disciplined on that too. Prolonged beatings and stuff basically same thing that I went through.

I got really angry about that. Susan would spank him. She usually used a wood spoon or sometimes the stick when he questioned them, or if he was disobedient, like whatever a normal kid does. Like playing with toys or stuff like that.

Both his parents used to beat him and when he wouldn't stop crying, they would beat him and tell him to stop crying or else he would get more. And of course, he didn't stop crying because he'd been beaten. This would go for at least two or three hours. They would beat him and send him to his room.

"He was usually hit on his back, sometimes on the back of his legs too. I saw bruises there and on his rear. It wasn't a spanking.

Susan had no problem doing it. She was following in my mother's footsteps quite happily. The last time I remember it was just before I left.

He would really listen to what I said, he showed really, quite a bit of intelligence. He used to tell me how much he hated his mother, how he wanted to kill her. My mom seemed to have a complete hold over him because he never told me anything about her, but he said how he wanted to kill his mother and describe in detail, which I found to be revolting. Being like, seven or eight years old.

And it was the hatred in him, just all hatred. Sometimes we would be friendly but when his mother would beat him and stuff like that, he lost everything, he lost all his conscience. And then he'd go out of his way to hurt animals. He'd do anything to hurt me.

He tried to beat me around the face or tried to punch me in the throat or whatever he could. He was a strong little kid too, but I never held it against him because I could tell, I saw him right away why it happened".

We were astounded that an eight-year-old child could plan to kill his mother and share his plans with Ricky. Langstaff continued and asked Ricky to expand on Nathaniel's plans.

"Well, ah sometimes, he would even like if he was holding

a bread knife or something, he'd whisper to me, um. How he would just like to cut his mother's face and kill her. I tried to instill something in him, I said you can't think that way, it's your mother."

Langstaff asked him if he had similar feelings towards his mother and his answer shocked us.

"Oh definitely. I still do, you know. What can you do?" he replied.

"Sometimes I'm sure everyone hates someone so much they can kill him but there are morals that get in the way: and there are laws that get in the way."

Langstaff asked about Ricky's anger and his violent thoughts.

"Oh, yah it's getting less, like I can push it away. I've always had to do that so I can do it here. Push my emotions away. But I've always wanted to get revenge but I'm not. I refused to give my life to get revenge for her because that way she would be winning. She would still be controlling my life".

"I might start to question her methods at other times. I felt rage and I guess maybe she saw that. I don't know what stopped me but then I would have destroyed her in her own way. A kid can only take so much and being fifteen or sixteen and I started to realize what was going on. The reason I always held myself in check because I was cursed by God and was going to Hell and then I'd have no chance".

"By that time, I knew that a lot of things she did was outside the law. And if I ever did anything to her, people would be pretty sympathetic, or I hoped they would".

His only concern was for the boy, Nathaniel, who was still living with his parents.

When I spoke with Ricky after his first interview at the school, I explained that the police could lay criminal charges against his mother for what she had done to him over the years.

"Now after what you have told me, I can take this to court. I can take your mother, the Pastor of this church, to court on these charges," I said.

He replied, "No, no, it doesn't matter what's happened to me in the past. I really don't have to go through that again. I just want to see Nathaniel get out of there." I couldn't persuade him to testify in court. I believed that this whole case might just collapse with this development.

However, the next day I received a phone call from Ricky's older brother Ron. Ron had explained to Ricky that he would be a witness and that this might be a way of helping himself to deal with this situation; that it might be good to go through with the court proceedings.

As a result, Ricky agreed to testify in court and my investigation continued.

4

Chapter 4

STATEMENT OF FAITH AND PRACTICE
OF
HIS REST CHRISTIAN FELLOWSHIP

The Pastor was not a Pastor, at least not in the eyes of the church proper. She was not an ordained Pastor but rather a self-proclaimed Pastor. She was a 56-year-old mother of three boys who raised them under the principles of the church she created and ran from her home. The family lived in an historic field stone house in an isolated area of Scarborough, far from the watchful eye of neighbours.

She created the Statement of Faith and Practice as a guide for behaviour and lifestyle by which all were to abide.

Passages included:

"We believe in the committed membership to the Lord and to the local expression of the body universal."

"Committed to a specific Church".

"Committed to the vision of the leadership in that Church."

"Committed in terms of time and energy to that Church."

"Committed to the meeting times of that Church."

"Committed in terms of financial support of that Church."

"Committed in a specific way to the membership of that Church."

"Committed to bearing the burdens of that Church."

Discipline:

"Discipline to be administered where there is a persistent following after the wrong ways of God."

"Discipline to exercised where there is a danger of harm to the rest of the family of God."

"Discipline is always administered with a view to restoration."

"Discipline has degrees."

Questions concerning membership:

"Who desires to become a member of this local Church?"

"Have you accepted Jesus Christ as your personal Lord and Saviour?"

"Do you know from the Lord that He is setting you into this local Church?"

"Do you know and understand the basic teachings of the Church?"

"Will you abide under the authority and discipline of the Elders whom the Lord has placed over this local Church?"

She encouraged her eldest son, Jeremy, to bring his school friends home with him to hear her teachings in an attempt to expose them to her belief system and lifestyle. This was short lived as his friends soon realized her ways were not for them.

She would often drive around and pick up hitchhikers in an attempt to increase her following. At times she had up to twenty-five people living in the home. She was even known to pick up Cambodian refugees.

Responding to a child abuse complaint from a former cult

member, The Toronto Children's Aid Society became involved with the Pastor and her family in December 1977.

The former member reported abuse of Nathaniel at the Pastor's home. He described the Pastor as the leader of a religious sect, stating she had total authority and claimed to be a Prophet.

The former member stated that the Pastor's son, Ron, had told him that the Pastor had beaten Nathaniel with an egg flipper. Sometimes the beatings would last 15-20 minutes. Ron told him that he had seen the black and blue bruises on Nathaniel's buttocks, as had the babysitter.

He advised that Doug was the Pastor's husband and co-leader of the sect. He further advised that Doug had been fired from his employment amid allegations of abuse involving special needs children.

The Toronto Children's Aid Worker contacted the Pastor and she and Greg, Nathaniel's adoptive father, attended for interviews.

The Pastor told the worker that Nathaniel was not Greg's biological child. She stated that Nathaniel was rebellious and disobedient as he had an evil spirit in him and therefore must be strictly disciplined.

The worker advised the Pastor of the serious bruising on Nathaniel's buttocks. Which the Pastor denied.

The worker noted that the Pastor was very controlling. The Pastor stated that "Greg is too weak to listen to and discuss allegations". When the worker insisted, he be interviewed, the Pastor became irate and over-controlling.

When the worker did interview Greg, he appeared upset but did not deny about the bruising. He stated that it was not severe and usually disappeared within a week. Greg advised the worker that it would not happen again.

The file was closed in March 1978.

In May 1983, Toronto Police attended at the Pastor's home in response to a report made by a Cambodian refugee who was living in the home. She reported that Nathaniel's parents, Greg, and Susan, had been beating her children.

The Youth Bureau Officers who attended advised the children appeared frightened. They had old marks and scars from their time in the refugee camp, but the officers were unable to validate any recent signs of abuse.

The case was therefore referred to The Toronto Children's Aid Society for follow-up. The worker interviewed the Cambodian mother who stated that they were being "misused by the church".

She supported that statement by advising the following:

They were paying $1100/month for rent.

The children had to attend private school which was run by the Church.

They had to denounce Buddhism to become Protestant.

They were not allowed to leave the farmhouse to join relatives in Montreal.

They were kept isolated from other Cambodians.

Her husband said he was going to forsake all and follow his Pastor as she told him that it was God's plan in bringing him to Canada.

The worker spoke to the Pastor's husband, Doug, who advised that the family was sponsored by the church under World Vision. Doug advised that they spoke no English and he was overseeing the schooling of the children and that it was administered by the Board of Education.

The worker interviewed Nathaniel's mother, Susan. Susan

was already known to Children's Aid due to a previous file relating to her husband Greg.

Susan stated that all of the allegations were false accusations by people strongly opposed to their faith.

After an investigation, the file was closed in December 1983.

5

Chapter 5

INCESTUOUS AFFAIRS

Ricky also told us about some *other things* his mother would do.

During the initial interview at the school, Langstaff asked Ricky if he had ever been sexually assaulted. He replied, "Yeah".

"It seems that, what you were, perhaps what happened was that your mother was trying to make you have intercourse with her?", Langstaff asked.

"I was about 13 or 14 by the time I reached puberty, and this is about when it started."

"My mom would come up to my room while I was being punished and I was asleep. She would wake me up and tell me about God's wrath. It was usually in the middle of the night. She liked to do that for some reason".

Ricky told us that his mother attempted to have intercourse with him on more than one occasion. Ricky refused her advances but said it would keep happening to him again without success.

He appeared uncomfortable and was evasive about answering

our questions. He appeared to be too humiliated to provide details.

Ricky appeared embarrassed. His body language changed. His head dropped …. his shoulders slumped…. he would not elaborate any further.

After a few moments of awkward silence, Langstaff asked, "When did it happen?

"Well, I don't know. It was tried, my mother tried. She didn't follow through with it, I was being a little sore."

Later in the interview, Langstaff asked Ricky if the discussion had hit a sore spot with him and if the attempts at incest were a result of God's word.

I interjected, "That it must be done or had to be done…. or… ?"

"Yah or basically if I did what if, or if I went against her, I was going against God, or whatever she said. And whatever she wanted me to do I didn't because I'm now going to Hell and I'd be burned," he said.

"But you would burn in Hell for not going along with her," I asked. "But that was basically with anything that she told you to do or wanted you to do. She had that tight of a reign on you?"

"Yah," he replied.

I asked Ricky how he was able to get it to stop.

"Well after a certain point, I guess she was afraid to, she could only go so far. I guess that maybe she saw that I was only going to take so much. And that I might start to question her methods. At other times I felt rage and I guess maybe she saw that. I don't know what stopped me but then I would destroy her in my own way".

"Again, a kid can only take so much, you know, fifteen or sixteen then, I was capable of doing it, you know that. But I always held myself in check 'cause ah, you know, I was cursed by God and was going to go to Hell and then I'd have no chance."

As the story unfolded and became more bizarre, I found myself wondering if he was being truthful. I had investigated a number of assault cases involving young people, but never did they follow an ongoing pattern of abuse *with* a mind control component.

As the interview progressed though my doubts were laid to rest. His body language spoke volumes and I could clearly see the pain and discomfort that he displayed. He slumped his shoulders and looked at the floor defeated.

Towards the end of the first interview, I asked Ricky if he had any scars as a result of his treatment at the hands of his mother.

He lifted up his shirt and revealed nine slash wounds, about two to three inches long, on his chest and upper body area that appeared to have healed on their own. There was no evidence of stitch marks. He also lowered his pants and I saw a three-inch wound on his left thigh that also did not appear to have been treated. Ricky told me that his mother had cut him with a box cutter to purify him and to rid him of the Devil.

I saw nine different healed cuts that appeared to me to be knife scars that were straight but at different angles that indicated to me that they were probably the result of slashing. The scars were on his back, chest and both thighs and the longest was eight to ten inches. I could not see any indication that the wounds had been stitched by a doctor. Ricky told me they had been left to heal on their own.

During a formal interview session with Ricky several days later, he described in more detail, the sexual assaults he had endured at the hands of his mother.

The words were spilling out of Ricky as he continued to

recount the abuse and beatings that would finally lead him to escape.

"In August of 1984, I was asleep in my room one night when my mother came into my room. She got into my bed and when I questioned, her, she said that she was going to have sexual intercourse with me. She told me it was God's way and that I was an ugly person and nobody else would, so she would have to have sex with me.

I refused and when that happened, she slashed me on the right side of my hip using a red box cutter knife. She would give her reasons for the cutting because if I did not perform, then she had to purify me by cutting me. I received no treatment for this wound.

In September of 1984, I got into an argument with my mother and her husband Doug, and I stormed out to a room where the phone was kept. I told them I was leaving and going to live with my dad. But my mother, Doug and two other church members held me down physically so I couldn't use the phone. They sat on top of me because I was kicking and fighting to break free. They held me for about an hour and my mother kept praying. Finally, when I calmed down, they took me to my room, and they watched me all night.

That same month, Ricky's mother had taken him to a friend's cottage. She waited until no one was home to make another advance on Ricky.

Ricky advised, "they took me to their friend's cottage to try to convert me back to her faith and stay at home. When Doug and the girl went into town, my mother again approached me to have sexual intercourse with her. Again, I refused. This time she used a kitchen knife on me. I was cut on the left shoulder, my lower back and chest. Again, I did not receive any treatment for this injury," he said.

Ricky stated, "And she would say how could I go to sleep when I was on the road to Hell, you know. It was quite scary actually. Because I believed everything she said. When I finally left home at 17, I was sure that God was going to strike me down and I was going to go to Hell before I even got into my father's place. But I said to myself, well, if I'm going to Hell, it can't be worse than this place. I'd sooner be there; somewhere where my mother isn't. So, I left anyways, and nothing happened."

"It was surprising to me even being 17 years old."

By November of 1984, Ricky finally escaped and went to live with his father.

Ricky told me that he had practiced jumping out of his bedroom window a few times before he tried his actual escape from his home. Then finally one night under the cover of darkness, he made his escape. Carrying some clothes with him he made the leap from his second-floor window.

Ricky carefully made his way through the forest at the side of the house. He waded through a small creek which brought him to the road where his father was waiting……. ready to take Ricky away from his years of abuse. The two had an emotional reunion.

During the same month, after having left his mother's home and, without his father's knowledge, Ricky returned to his mother's home to retrieve some clothes and some personal belongings. She was the only one in the home.

"I was inside the house talking to my mother and again she started at me to have intercourse with her.Again, I refused, and she used the same razorblade knife on me. She went crazy and slashed my left upper arm and down onto my left upper thigh. I left and I have not been back since.""She did try to get me back though.She would call day and night until we finally changed our number to an unlisted number".

Ricky was finally free and had no intentions of ever going back.

6

Chapter 6

THE EXORCISMS

The family had lived in two houses when the boys were growing up. They first resided in Scarborough (a suburb of Toronto) before moving to an old stone farmhouse in Pickering (a city located east of Toronto) when Ron was about 11 years old.The house they were renting was sold and was slated to be torn down for development.

Ron recalled that his older brother, Jeremy, had brought a number of friends to the Scarborough home for Bible studies and they were joined by others he described as "down and outers" who had nowhere else to go. The students soon tired of the teachings from the Pastor but others remained as permanent residents for longer periods of time.

He recalled that his mother's behaviour changed for the worse after the move.

They were later joined by a man named Doug, who would eventually leave his wife and begin living as husband to the Pastor.

"He did quite well for himself, and I know he turned over a large portion of his income to the cause and so did other people when they were expected to this and, um, there was no accounting for the money, of course," Ron explained.

"Tithing, which is based on a biblical principle that 10 percent of your money goes to God. Well, although I'm not certain of the amounts turned over to my mother, obviously things had to be financed. My mother's ministry, "His Rest Christian Fellowship", had to be financed somehow and my mother didn't bring any money in," Ron stated.

I asked him how the services were conducted, other than his mother's sermon to them.

"Yah, they had deliverance services that were called exorcisms. I've seen a couple of those services take place and they were quite scary. I was just 11 then. I remember Ricky and I sitting on the staircase coming down from the bedrooms to the living room area and seeing the person.

The person would be in the middle of the group on a chair or standing up and everyone would lay hands on them and begin praying, casting our certain demons. I've seen people start to flail about on the floor, literally, and even spewing a black bile out of their mouths and they'd make animal noises.

Anyone in the group could be exorcized when my mother deemed it to be necessary to be delivered and some people volunteered. It would sometimes take hours. I've seen that go on for hours. I can remember my brother Ricky and I going to bed, and they would continue afterwards. It was quite scary for us, you know, to hear this when we were upstairs."

I remember thinking that children should be peering through the stair railings waiting for Santa or watching their parents enjoy an evening with friends instead of watching exorcisms.

One of the participants that Ron particularly remembered was a friend of his who went to a local high school and was a star athlete.

"Yah that was incredible. He had to be restrained on the floor by several adults because he started flailing about. He was making noises that were very spooky. It looked like he was having an epileptic seizure and he spewed the black bile out of his mouth.

I think it was, as my mother put it, the evil spirit manifesting itself in him and of course we believed it at the time."

Ron reflected, "I can remember an incident with Nathaniel, who would have been about a year and a half old. Before Greg moved in with my mother full time, he brought his son Nathaniel for a visit. He started crying and my mother insisted Greg discipline him. My mother got a plastic spatula and insisted on spanking the child on the bare bottom. Greg started out and then my mother took over and this lasted for roughly twenty minutes, and they kept beating the back of his legs and his rear end. There were a lot of marks.

And the kid just kept screaming at the top of his lungs. My mother said he had to be taught at an early age to respect authority, respect his father and do as he's told. I can remember the marks the next day."

Ron and Ricky were normal boys. They fell off their bikes and had falls but they were never given any medical treatment.

Ron remembered one incident involving Ricky that stood out when we talked.

"He had a really bad toothache, and he was practically screaming in bed and my mother would not take him to a dentist. I believe she gave him an aspirin to chew on or something and they prayed for him, but he was in bad shape, I can remember that. It went on for a couple of days."

Although their biological father had moved away, Ron was becoming desperate to leave. At the tender age of 14 he made his move.

"I was camping at a park with some friends. They would sort of, uh, they would always talk sense into me about my father. Anyway, I was really getting to the point where I was questioning what was going on at the farm. I was old enough at 14.

I told them I wanted to speak to my father, so I called him long distance from the campground. I spoke to him, and he was delighted to hear from me, and I made an arrangement. I needed to see him for him to pick me up, but he wanted to arrange that I get my brother out as well. But my father wanted me to make a go of it at the farm so he could also get my brother out.

I came home that night and they interrogated me over what happened at the park. They wanted to know everything that went on. I just got so sick and tired that this is when I told myself I was going to make my break.

I told them that was it and I was going to live with my father. But they physically restrained me from leaving. Doug held the door shut on me. He physically held me, but I just yanked the door open and ran out.

My father was waiting at the bottom of the drive. I had taken a few belongings and I remember there was an incident at the bottom of the drive.

Doug yelled at my father that he and my mother forgave him even though he had never met him before. Then he called my dad a liar in front of us. He said he was an evil man and that he was a liar and a hypocrite."

Ron had made his move and had broken away.

Ron recalled that after he began to live with his father, his older brother, Jeremy, came back to Canada from Spain where he was serving as a Missionary. Both boys travelled to the farm where their mother was living. They tried to speak to Ricky however, they were met in the lane by their mother.

"I was standing behind my brother and we were talking to my mother.

All of a sudden, I saw my brother's sunglasses go flying off. My mother started striking my brother in the head, so I came in between them, and my mother struck me about three or four times very hard in the face and the head. So, we retreated behind a hedge, but we didn't leave which kind of surprised her.

She thought we would run off with our tails between our legs, but we waited while she called the police. When the officers arrived, they just told us to leave and that was the end of that."

Unknown to the boys, Ricky was standing at a window on the second floor of the house watching all that had happened.

Carolyn's hand drawing of the Scarborough House in 1986

Chapter 7

THOUGHTS SO FAR

I realized I was fighting a criminal who acted as if she was a direct conduit to God.

I turned my mind to how I was going to take the volume of information that I obtained so far in the investigation and start to prepare a case that would ensure everyone understood the depth of what had actually taken place.

A properly prepared criminal case does not happen like you see on television. There are a number of witnesses to interview, research to conduct into the functioning of cults, and statements to prepare.

All this takes time.

Proper procedures dictated that once I had all my facts, the Crown Attorney's office would become involved. This is the branch of the justice system whose lawyers prosecute criminal cases.

Throughout my investigation a common thread was emerging from my interviews with witnesses.

I could not simply deal with investigating a religion, as it's not against the law to have your own religion or whatever religion you want to worship or what God you want to pray to. There comes a point, however, when the actions involve criminal activity that the police and the criminal justice system definitely get involved.

My supervisory Detective had ordered me to devote all of my time to the case but without the resources I needed, I was on my own. Was I fighting religion while trying to establish a solid criminal case? Was Ricky's mother a Devil or in her mind was she just trying to help?

I also understood from Ricky that the cult had been investigated before by the Children's Aid Society and the police by using what I called the "front door method."

With this method, the Children's Aid Society calls ahead and makes an appointment for a home visit versus an unannounced visit. When they arrive at the door, the home presents as neat and tidy…. a "normal" family home.

Ricky had explained to us that had he been beaten, and the marks were evident, he would be sure not to be at home upon the arrival of police or the Children's Aid worker.Alternatively, he was placed in his room where he would stay and not be permitted to come out during the interview.

If it was a day when he had no marks, he was allowed to come downstairs. This held true when any guest or visitor came to the house.

Ricky was allowed to have a conversation with police and/or the Children's Aid worker but when it got to a point where it became a serious question, something he couldn't handle or got too sensitive for him to handle, he would simply reply, "Ask my mother".

He had been programmed to respond in this fashion to anyone in authority, or any adult visitor.

The facts in the case were becoming all too clear. This case had all the elements of criminal acts against children. I believed at least two of the children had been kept without the necessities of life and were physically assaulted as punishment for little or no reason. In several instances, attempts were made to sexually assault and commit incest against Ricky.

8

Chapter 8

FORMER MEMBERS COME FORWARD

I interviewed former members of the cult who were to be potential witnesses and who could corroborate the boys' stories of abuse. Their statements were either accurately recorded in my notes or were made in their own handwriting. I do recall that when speaking with these former members, they were happy and full of life, and so glad to be out of the church.

One of the original nine members of the "His Rest Christian Fellowship" served as a deacon and treasurer. He recalled the membership met Sunday afternoon and evening and Wednesday and Friday evenings "without fail".

"At these meetings we would discuss biblical teachings and listen to the Pastor's sermon. If you disagreed with any of her teachings, you were berated and told you had a demon of some kind and had to be delivered or you were no longer allowed at the meetings.

Friday nights were our prayer and deliverance meetings which meant if the fellowship felt one of the others had a demon or if an outsider came within us, they must be cleansed of demons before they could stand pure before God.

On a regular basis I witnessed normal, happy people pushed to the ground and held there until they were delivered. This would last until 4 a.m.

The Pastor was the law, and she would hold the reins on you very tightly and convince you that you were doing the will of God. If you followed her teachings, you were promoted to the fellowship."

There were lots of sugar snacks handed out during these prayer sessions which would deliver a sugar high and a sugar low. This, combined with the atmosphere of a hot stone farmhouse, for hours on end, added to the mental breakdown of a person to submit to the Pastor's control.

He explained that the weekly income from the cult's members was between $75 and $100 per person, of which most went straight to the Pastor's pocket to spend as she saw fit. She never issued a receipt for her expenses nor was any of it claimed for income tax purposes; it was just found money.

"The Pastor was always very hard on her boys at the time of my involvement. She was extremely hard on her oldest son, but I also saw her on more than one occasion, hit the other two brothers with force. But when there were others around, they were her little angels.

I remember one night we delivered one young black kid of all his demons and the next weekend he killed himself. That's how much power and intensity she had. She screwed up so many young people. She is a very strong-willed woman and one of the best con ladies I've ever seen.

I have a slight hearing impairment because when I was being delivered for demons, I was smacked in the ears or the face.

I was also choked to the point I was coughing up blood and mucous."

He also participated in a deliverance of up to eight hours nonstop where arm bending to the point of breaking a bone occurred.

"I've seen little Ricky, who was eight years old at the time, hit so hard that he flew across the room, and I saw the middle brother Ron beaten for religious infractions."

He noted that Ricky, "complained frequently about headaches and had problems seeing clearly with his eyes. He wanted to see an optometrist to get fitted for glasses but was denied by his mother. She felt that he should pray and trust God for the healing of his eyes. He said that he has prayed many times and his eyes were still the same".

He recalled that when Ricky was about 17 years old, he, "climbed out his window one night and ran across the roof and jumped. He was caught and brought into a small building which was attached to the main house. He was sat down in a corner, to the farthest corner away from the door, and six people were around him trying to convince him that what he was doing was wrong and that he shouldn't leave. A few days later he did escape."

"I can verify anyone who says they're a member either by sight, by name, or by talking to them for five minutes. The Pastor's teachings are ingrained in me even to this day."

The second person on my interview list was Nancy. Nancy's daughter Julie had been attending the Pastor's prayer meetings at the farmhouse. Nancy first observed one-year-old Nathaniel in a crib at the farmhouse. Approximately one month later, Nathaniel's father called and asked if she would look after Nathaniel "for a while", stating he would pay her $25/week.

Nancy agreed and became Nathaniel's sole caregiver for a year, with only a few quick short visits from Greg on Tuesdays and Saturdays. Nancy recalled, "when he first came to me, I thought that he could use a good scrub and clean up. He looked much better after the first week".

Nancy recalled that in the spring of 1978, Nathaniel's father, Greg, took him for an overnight visit. When he returned the next day, she saw immediately that Nathaniel was behaving strangely.

"When Greg brought him into the house, I noticed he was acting strange and looked guilty. Nathaniel seemed exhausted but I felt his diaper and it was dry, so I put him straight to bed.

The next morning when I took off his diaper, I noticed his entire rear end was a purple colour. I couldn't believe it so I took Nathaniel to a friend's house and showed her, and we both believed that somebody must have hit him. There was even one spot where the skin was broken, and I put Vaseline on it for several days. It took at least two weeks before the bruising went away.

When I found Nathaniel's injury, I called Greg at home. I told him to come over that night after work because I had something to show him. Greg came over about 5:00 and I showed him Nathaniel's injury and asked if he hit Nathaniel. He said no but that Nathaniel was playing with the boys. I said they must have used a two by four. Greg said I think he fell down a hill. I told Greg I didn't believe him and that if I had proof, I would report him, if it was him that hit Nathaniel".

In the summer of 1978 Nathaniel went back to his parents. Some time later, Julie told her that it was actually the Pastor who had hit Nathaniel with a wooden spoon.

Nancy did not see him for about a year until a chance

encounter. She recalled, "Nathaniel looked very sad and was quiet. He seemed to cling to Greg and didn't look good."

That was the last time she saw Nathaniel.

My next interview was with Julie, Nancy's daughter. Julie, who was a member of the cult, recalled several instances of abuse involving physical assaults. One in particular she recounted to police.

"Nathaniel was maybe one or two. She took a spatula, those plastic ones, and you could hear that she was hitting him. I remember someone else at the lunch table went outside crying. She couldn't handle it.

But nobody would say anything because she knows what she's doing, after all she cries when she prays and calls up on the name of the Lord, and how could she be wrong, you know.

So that lasted about 45 minutes, the spanking. Then she came out and she looked like she's been labouring, and she wanted us to feel sorry for her. She came out as a martyr, like, and she held her stomach and she blew up and she said this kid is rebellious, like her favourite word is rebellious.

She told her husband to go in the room to help her. She told him she was labouring spanking this kid and you're not doing a thing. There was more of that spanking, a lot of yelling, telling Nathaniel to behave and he was not going to get away with this."

My witnesses required a significant amount of guidance and reassurance that the information they were now providing me was a major part of this complicated investigation.I assured them that important information comes from a variety of sources. Many people think that what they know may not make a difference as they don't feel that they know a lot about a situation.

I told them that even small pieces of information, like a puzzle, comes together to make one big picture. Their bravery in sharing their experiences would help me put the pieces of this investigation together and would help two very fragile young boys immensely.

Their information corroborated what I had learned from Ricky about the children's beatings, their deprivation from food and nourishment and their isolation of being locked in their rooms.

They were an asset in helping to prove my case.

Chapter 9

THE SEARCH WARRANT

I was pumped!

The Criminal Code of Canada states that in order for police to enter a private home or business to conduct a search, they have to have a valid reason and the reason must be laid out in writing to a Justice of the Peace (JP). The JP has similar powers to a Criminal Court Judge. The JP is responsible for making a decision as to whether or not to permit police to enter a premise to search for evidence of the commission of a crime. If the JP is satisfied that the police have presented enough grounds, the JP may then sign the Warrant to Search.

My investigation and case preparation necessitated the application for two search warrants. I was requesting permission from the court to search the homes in Scarborough and Pickering where I believed the offences had taken place.

On my Pickering warrant application, I stated that I was looking for sticks, pieces of lumber or weapons such as the red handled box cutter that Ricky had earlier described to me as the weapon the Pastor cut him with and used in his discipline. I did not have an exact address for the house in Pickering and so, with the assistance of several Durham Regional Police Service Officers, we drove to the general area described to us by Ricky. We caught a break because the Pastor's home had a nice big mailbox at the side of the road with her name on it.

The JP granted my application for the search warrant for the Pickering location.

With respect to the Scarborough warrant, the JP was having trouble deciding if there was enough information listed to substantiate the issuance of a warrant, given the passage of time since the offences had taken place. The JP asked me if there was anything else that I was searching for in addition to the weapons, such as items pertaining to the existence of a religious cult.

I had nothing!

At that moment, I remembered a conversation with an officer from 42 Division who had been recently dispatched to a Scarborough field for a call unrelated to my investigation. That investigation required him to contact the police division and he attended a nearby home for that purpose. A woman answered and let him in to use her phone. The officer noticed a young boy, about ten years of age, in the home. The officer also noticed stacks of religious pamphlets scattered throughout the home.

The officer made a second call .... to me.

"Hey Dave," he said. "I remember you had said something at the station about your investigation into this religious cult. Well, I'm at a house in east Scarborough that has a lot of religious information, and I was wondering if they are associated to your cult?"

"What are their names?" I asked. When he told me, my heart jumped to my mouth.

"Is there a ten-year-old boy there?", I said. When he said there was and that he appeared to be in good health, I knew it was Nathaniel.

As the officer was leaving, Nathaniel's mother handed him a red Bible stamped with the name of His Rest Christian Fellowship. By sheer chance he had stumbled upon the home of one of the main participants in the Pastor's cult.

That was more than enough for the JP.

The search warrants were granted and were to take place on July 9th.

The Toronto Children's Aid Society had also been successful in obtaining a Warrant of Apprehension for Nathaniel. All addresses had been confirmed and both the Toronto Police Service and Durham Regional Police Service teams had been assigned.

We were good to go, and we held a pre-raid meeting with, as it turned out, nearly 30 people from two law enforcement agencies as well as the Toronto and Durham Children's Aid Societies attended.

It was crucial that we attended at the two houses at the same time, especially when the Children's Aid Societies were looking for the young boy to take him into their custody. If we attended one house at a time, and if the boy was not there, a cult member could make a phone call to the second home, and we would never find him!

One of the Toronto Police Service uniformed officers on my team was none other that the Pastor's middle son Ron. Who better to bring along with me to positively identify his mother if she was at the home? Over the years, Ron had completely distanced himself from his mother when he left to live with his father, and he was completely blindsided by the details of this investigation.

We arrived at the Pastor's home in Durham Region at about 6:00 pm. I knocked at the front door of this old field stone house and was met by a woman who identified herself as Nathaniel's mother Susan. She told me the Pastor was away in California at a religious meeting and was not available.

I thought to myself, "Well I'll be damned.... you know.... here they prepare for the day of the Anti-Christ.... I arrive and they're not home...."

I identified myself to her, served her with a copy of the search warrant and explained why we had come.

We stepped inside the foyer. The atmosphere changed. It was like stepping into the past.

The air was dusty, and sunbeams were attempting to cut through the bleak stale air. An oppressive heaviness hung in the air.... like a window hadn't been open in ages.

I was taken aback by Susan's appearance. She was dressed like a 19th century pioneer woman. Her dress was full length and made of ragged cotton; her movements stirred up the dust on the floor. As she stood at the bottom of the staircase, I could see that her face was pasty white.She was like a ghostly apparition from the movies.

I placed her under arrest with respect to her role in the offences against Nathaniel and turned her over to a uniformed officer.

There were more than ten rooms in the two-storey house that had to be searched in addition to the basement.

There were several other uniform officers from Durham Regional Police Service with me and we divided the house into search segments.

Clutter was everywhere.

There were stacks of religious pamphlets and personal diaries on tables, on desks, on the floor …. practically on any flat surface in the house…. making movement and searching difficult.

The major portion of my warrant was to search for and seize items such as sticks that may have been used to beat the boys. I was also anxious to find the box cutter knife that Ricky described as being used by the Pastor to cut him when he refused to take part in any sexual activities with her.

I observed tree branches in various locations throughout the house that looked like walking sticks. Some were leaning up against the walls and some were laying on the floor. Strangely, many of the sticks appeared to be hand carved and had names etched into them. Every few minutes, an officer would come to me with another stick or box cutter knife he had discovered in one of the rooms he had searched. It seemed as if every room had its share of primitive weapons.

I stood at the top the basement stairs looking down. Each stair appeared solid but well worn from years of use. Looking into the basement, the air appeared as heavy and dusty as I had first observed in the front foyer. Along the side of the staircase was a wooden shelf, heavily laden with various types of preserves. Each glass jar was massive; at least a gallon and they were stockpiled.

Were they preparing to do battle with the Anti-Christ?

As I descended the staircase into the basement, I observed that there was only one very low wattage bulb to illuminate the entire basement. The floor was dirt, and the stone walls gave off a dank, musty old smell and feel that was chilling to

53

the bone. There were bags of dried herbs hanging from the beams and held together by the heavy cobwebs that clung to them. With the use of my flashlight, I observed three rooms each stockpiled with commercial sized cans of food and more jarred preserves. Truth be told, my heart skipped a beat before I opened each of the freezers I found down there.

We had been searching for about an hour, but I still wasn't satisfied that I had found *the* knife used in the attacks on Ricky. The search was painstaking, it was hot in the house, and I was getting frustrated. I radioed to Ron and asked if he could assist in providing a more detailed description of the box cutter I was searching for. Ron described the box cutter as painted red with the Pastor's name written on it, and that it would possibly be in a leather suitcase used for leather work. I continued my search of the basement.

I had just about given up when, in a dark corner of one the rooms, I spotted a battered leather suitcase standing all on its own. The leather had been painted white and the suitcase had wide leather buckle straps. I was hopeful upon opening the suitcase.

Contained inside were many pieces of cut leather and leather working tools. I rummaged around inside the suitcase and found what I believed to be *the* red painted box cutter knife. I breathed a sigh of relief. When I turned around and showed the two Durham Detectives Sturgeon and McKechnie what I had found, we did a little happy dance.

Everything Ricky had told us about the abuse was now solidly backed up by physical evidence.

When I came up from my search of the basement, I observed that uniformed officers had detained, who I believed to be, cult members. They were not questioning or upset about what we were doing, as is the norm during a search warrant. In fact, they appeared dazed and zombie like and were as pale as Susan. They seemed indifferent to *our* presence in *their* home.

I opened the front door and the feeling of fresh air and summer warmth returned me to the present from the oppressive 19th century feel of the home.

Chapter 10

NATHANIEL

Nathaniel jumped into the back seat of the Children's Aid Society's vehicle without question. Nathaniel was driven back to 42 Division in company with Lynn Factor, and Russ McFawn, Durham Children's Aid Society workers.

During the ride they began a taped conversation with Nathaniel.

"So, are you anxious to see Ricky?" Lynn asked.

"Yes, it would be nice to see him again. I want to see my mom too. Yeh, like my mom and dad are divorced. My mom and dad, like this one here, Redhead I call him, and my other dad (Greg), he's working overtime today, they aren't my real dad. My real dad's Indian and my real mom is in Nova Scotia. I have part Indian in me," he said.

Russ asked Nathaniel what happened when he got into trouble at home.

"Like only once this happened. My mom didn't know what to do so she phoned my dad. That's when I was grounded for four days. I just had to stay in my room, nothing to eat. Nothing.

I had good meals, like my friend snuck it in there. Don't tell mom and dad that he snuck it in 'cause he'd be in real trouble. He snuck me in pop and everything. He'd do go down to Becker's Milk Store and buy me stuff."

He told them his parents had not brought him any food for the four days. He admitted, however, that he had a stockpile from his friend, so he didn't ask for any.

As Nathaniel lived in the same home as the Pastor, Russ asked him what the Pastor did to him if he made her angry.

"Um, she really doesn't bug me anymore. She grounded me once. That's the only time. Sometimes she would spank you on the rear end with a small stick or a wooden spoon."

"Does it hurt?" Nathaniel was asked.

"Of course. Is it ever sore", he replied

At approximately 10:30 pm, Lynn Factor and I commenced an audiotaped statement with Nathaniel. I was interested in learning more about Nathaniel's life with his parents and with the Pastor. Lynn began the interview by determining if Nathaniel understood the meaning of the word discipline.

"Well, I haven't had much discipline this year but last year, if I was really bad, I'd get a good swat and if it was just something small, I had to write out lines. If my parents found out I swore or something like that, I'd get a swat. Either my mom or dad. Whoever found out first."

Nathaniel told us they had used a wooden spoon for discipline.

He also told us about the lack of any medical care given to him.

He had never seen a doctor or dentist.

"I went to my teacher's house I was going to pet her cat and suddenly it looked at me and the Devil got into it or something and shhhhhhh like this, eh I go, ouch, right and put her down and I feel my eye go all blurry and I felt a pain right there.

I went home and someone asked what happened to my eye so I told her and she takes me to the bathroom and wipes it off, right. And she put some iodine on it. It was bleeding and my eye hurt and she put some cotton stuff on it, and I went to bed."

Lynn asked why he didn't go to a doctor.

"I don't know. They didn't want to pay for it or something like that. It hurt for a few weeks. I mean it took a good chunk out of it. You can see there's still a chunk out of it."

When asked about seeing a dentist, he said he had never been to one.

"It's too crowded at the bottom of my mouth. They usually hurt when I eat. Like if I eat something hard like potatoes. That's pretty soft but it hurts."

Nathaniel had told his parents but there was no help given.

"I say my teeth hurt. They said they will pray but it doesn't help actually. I say come next time and say my teeth hurt and they say they will pray, and I said it didn't help last time. They just told me to try the next time. I thought to myself 'Ah come on I can't endure the pain that long".

It appeared to us that Nathaniel was a lonely little boy with few friends.

"I'm allowed to read comics. But I mean I don't have stacks of comics, like I go through a book in half an hour. You'd have problems stocking me with books. I. Well I have some friends, but they aren't near. I don't see them every day; they're like my best friends almost".

Loneliness was an issue for Nathaniel.

"I feel lonely sometimes. It'd be different if I had my real mom and dad with me, you know it'd be different. I'd have brothers and sisters and stuff, and they'd live in the community, and I'd go to public school and stuff."

Like any little boy, Nathaniel had his fair share of bumps and bruises. Except his were never treated. He remembered that when he was seven years old, his mother accidentally spilled scalding soup on his shirt sleeve.

"I was stunned right, and if I wasn't so dumb, I would have pulled it off and I wouldn't have been burnt."

Clearly Nathaniel had been conditioned to believe that everything, including a severe injury, was his own fault.

The only treatment he described was his mother wrapping the burn with some kind of cloth to stop any infection. He was never taken to a doctor. When it was healing the burn blistered and Nathaniel was afraid to move his arm in case the blister burst. Several days later, the Pastor stuck it with a needle, and it burst.

I noticed a scar on Nathaniel's left knuckle and asked him what had happened.

He said he was using a large knife to cut a bun when it slipped and cut his hand down to the bone. His parents weren't home so a woman, who was a cult member, put tobacco and brown sugar on it and wrapped it in a cloth. He was never taken for medical treatment.

I showed him the sticks and the knife that we had recovered, and he identified them as some of the weapons that had been used to inflict beatings on him. One of the sticks was carved by Nathaniel as a present for his stepmother Susan. Susan in turn used it as a weapon against him.

It was close to 11:30 p.m. when we finished the interview. Nathaniel was taken to an emergency foster home, and he never went back with his parents, Susan, and Greg, again.

During the drive to the foster home, Nathaniel, who had been through a long and exhausting process, asked only two questions. "Will there be a television? Will I be allowed to visit my birth mother?"

On January 22, 1987, Nathaniel was professionally assessed. Excerpts from that report noted the following:

- On two occasions in the residence Nathaniel has dealt with built up feelings in an aggressive manner
- He has hit staff twice and used abusive violent language a number of times.
- Twice restraints and aggression programs were necessary.
- He acts as though he is joking or playing but can become verbally and physically very hurtful and aggressive.
- He is becoming increasingly manipulative and tries to get around homework.
- His homework book was assigned to counter the problem, but he works at getting around that.
- At these times he will adamantly deny and gives lengthy explanations and avoids further discussion and eye contact
- He has been late for school several times without reason.
- He has been caught smoking at school.
- The school is aware of at least three fistfights.
- Great difficulty in accepting responsibility and will protest that he is not at fault and had good reason to act as he has.
- Has aches and pains.
- Nathaniel's parents have told him that the family had left the church as a result of his apprehension and that they will go to prison as a result of the statements he made.
- Confusion over why he was beaten.

- Nathaniel talked about witches, full moons, and were-wolves and that they would meet in a park, on a full moon, and these people would turn into vicious animals.
- He explained that these people are Satan worshipers and this he had learned through his parents.
- Nathaniel's birth mother had not followed through on any visits with him.
- She let it be known that she was going through difficulties in her life at the moment and needed to sort that out first.

A further report on January 27, 1987, indicated:

- Altercations with other children
- Lying to the staff and to the school staff
- Not completing 15 or 16 assignments and lying about it
- Very little motivation – does not want to follow routines.
- Nathaniel is holding in a great deal of his feelings and rather than dealing with them is acting out.
- Long history of bed wetting and hides his wet sheets and pyjamas.
- Nathanial stated that he wets the bed when he has night-mares.
- Extremely quiet and reserved.
- Establishes little eye contact during any session and only speaks when answering a question.

In February 1987, the Children's Aid Society of Durham Region took part in a custody hearing for Nathaniel to determine if he would be returned to his parents, Susan, and Greg. The primary witness was Ricky who, by this time, had been living with his father full time.

The hearing lasted for a number of hours. Suddenly at one point, Susan, and Greg, with their lawyer present declared that they were no longer interested in fighting for custody of Nathaniel.

You could have heard a pin drop.

Upon becoming aware of the outcome of Nathaniel's custody hearing, the Pastor's son, Ron, commented to me, "basically what they had done was on the orders of the Pastor like, well we lost that one, that's okay you know, we'll send one sheep to slaughter to save the whole flock".

11

Chapter 11

THE CASE COMES TOGETHER

Further research on my part indicated that members put their money from their regular jobs into the pot which went to the church.

They all lived with the Pastor and attended prayer meetings which lasted between eight and ten hours. I learned that they were not fed during the meetings however there was a lot of candy being consumed.

It turns out that this is a trick used by cult recruiters around the world.

The scheme was to deprive the participants of food but provide them lots of candy to ensure a sugar high. The participants, already fatigued by the duration of meeting, were almost to the point of exhaustion. They were now at the mercy of the Pastor and her religious indoctrination.

My interviews with them were extremely difficult. By finally leaving the cult, attending another church, and speaking with a Minister of another faith, they realized that the Pastor's teachings and lifestyle had not been the norm.

The cult had consumed them and their lives for a number of years.

I reflected on the many hours and days spent conducting interviews, ensuring that I had done my very best to get all the information that I would need to present a strong case. CAS worker Lynn Factor and I spent copious amounts of time painstakingly listening to all of the audio recordings of all the victim and witness interviews to ensure a correct representation of the facts. In addition, countless more hours were spent by one clerk Linda, who was entrusted to transcribe all the interviews for court purposes.

As the Detective Constable in charge of the investigation, I met with several Crown Attorneys during the case preparation process to discuss the facts of the case, the appropriate charges to lay and the best way to proceed in court. Often during this process, the Crown Attorney who originally consults is not the same Crown Attorney that is present at trial.It can be a tiring process to have to start all over again when I had a question or needed clarification. My role was also to assist and advise the Crown Attorney during the court trials.

Crown Attorneys are lawyers who act on behalf of the citizens of Canada and, in fact, represent the Queen, hence the name Crown Attorney. Their rules of operation, as are those of the courts and the police, are laid out in the Criminal Code of Canada, which is a book that defines all criminal offences in the Canadian Justice System.

The Crown Attorney took into consideration the information obtained from Greg's post arrest statement. Susan, however, gave no statement but talked on the phone with a cult member for the duration of her time in custody until being released that evening for a future court date.

The Pastor declined to be interviewed on the advice of her counsel. She sat in the interview room chanting, saying prayers, and singing hymns.

Detective Constable McManus conducted Greg's interview and the following is an excerpt of that interview.

Greg denied any knowledge of specific assaults.

McManus asked, "If you found it necessary to discipline him, for misbehaving, by what means would you do it?"

Greg replied, "I normally use a wooden spoon to spank him."

McManus asked, "Where do you normally hit him with the spoon?"

"Only on his seat", he replied, then quickly backtracked, and attempted to clarify his statement by saying, "I wouldn't say normally, it's just a very rare occurrence."

Greg confirmed that Nathaniel had never been taken to a doctor for any injuries he may have had, nor had he ever been taken to a dentist stating, "because I am a Christian and I believe in divine healing when you pray for it."

When asked about other forms of discipline, Greg confirmed that he had sent Nathaniel to his room and, "he would usually miss a meal", then backtracked once again to say, "he wouldn't actually miss a meal, he would only have a light meal".

The Crown Attorney and I worked for two days before coming up with an appropriate set of charges to be proceeded with against the Pastor, her husband Doug, and Nathaniel's parents, Susan, and Greg.

The charges laid were as follows:

1.Failure to Provide the Necessities of Life with respect to Ricky, over a period spanning 1975 to 1985.

- Charges laid against the Pastor and Doug.

2.Assault with a Weapon with respect to an assault committed against Ricky using a three-foot-long tree branch.

-Charges laid against the Pastor and Doug.

3.Two charges of Counselling to Commit Incest relating to the Pastor's 1984 efforts to have intercourse with her son Ricky.

-Charges laid against the Pastor.

4.Two charges of Sexual Assault relating to the Pastor's 1984 attempts to have intercourse with her son Ricky.

-Charges laid against the Pastor.

5.Two charges of Aggravated Assault for the use of a box cutter on Ricky when he refused to have sex with the Pastor.

-Charge laid against the Pastor.

6.Two charges of Weapons Dangerous with respect to her use of a box cutter on Ricky.

-Charge laid against the Pastor.

7.Fail to Provide the Necessities of Life and Assault

-Charges laid against Susan and Greg (Nathaniel's parents)

12

Chapter 12

THE TRIALS BEGIN

The Canadian justice system provides for two types of criminal trials. Minor criminal cases are heard in the Provincial Court and are conducted in front of a Provincial Court Justice.

The more serious cases are heard in the Superior Court of Justice, formerly known as the Supreme Court of Ontario, where the trial is either held in front of a Superior Court Justice alone, who hears the evidence and renders a verdict, or the accused person may elect to have their trial conducted in front of a Superior Court Justice and a jury.

When the accused person is slated for a Superior Court trial, the law dictates that they may first appear in front of a Provincial Judge in what is termed a 'preliminary inquiry'. At this point, it is up to the Provincial Court Judge to determine if the Crown Attorney has presented enough evidence to warrant a trial in front of the Superior Court. An accused person may select to bypass the preliminary inquiry and go directly to the Superior Court.

Susan and Greg waived their right to have a preliminary inquiry and chose to proceed directly to trial before a Judge alone at the Scarborough Court.

The Scarborough Court is located in a suburb of Toronto and occupies most of a large strip mall. This court location handles criminal trials for adults and young offenders as well as hears traffic ticket proceedings.

I was always fascinated by the cross section of humanity that presented itself there. Hardened criminals would rub shoulders with first time offenders, speeders, young offenders, police, lawyers, and spectators who came to watch the trials to pass time.

Police officers find themselves in a unique situation when they prepare a criminal case and are ready to take it to court for trial. The officer's investigation is often scrutinized, interpreted, and turned around by law firms whose sole purpose is to attempt to find inconsistencies in the investigation.

Statements, like the ones I took from Ricky and Nathaniel at the beginning of the case, are examined word for word and defence lawyers often try to trip them up. They may imply the witness was lying or had been coached by the police or the crown attorney to give their evidence in a certain way that lends credibility to the crown's case.

This often occurs with sexual assault cases where the defence attempts to present the victim as a person who is lying about the offence or, perhaps, they agreed to all the acts implied and are just getting even. The victim is required to bare their soul in case the defence can catch them in a lie or characterize the victim as someone who is just trying to get revenge for the sexual assault.

On many an occasion at trial, a witness or victim may recall and disclose an event or detail that was not disclosed during the investigation, not through any malice or intent to mislead. Sometimes the line of questioning simply brings a previously undisclosed detail to light.

On April 9th and 10th, 1987 the trial commenced in Scarborough Court against Susan and Greg who were charged with Assault and Failing to Provide the Necessities of Life. I was confident in having Crown Attorney Karen Dunlop assigned to the case.

As expected, the first person who testified was Ricky. Although he was nervous, he was very consistent with his testimony.

Ricky told the Judge how he came to know Susan and Greg, when they became part of the church and what their roles were within the church.

He testified that their son, Nathaniel, was approximately two years old when he came to the home. Ricky recalled Nathaniel's abuse at the hands of Susan and Greg.

The first incident he recounted for the court was one of Susan beating Nathaniel in the bathroom. The door was left open, giving Ricky a clear vantage point from where he stood in the kitchen. Susan was using a spatula, or a wooden stick, for about 20 minutes off and on, on Nathaniel's lower back, backside, and the lower back of his legs. She was striking him hard.

Nathaniel was screaming, crying, and squirming to escape.Ricky testified that all this occurred as a reprimand for Nathaniel being outside.

Ricky advised that Nathaniel was sent to his room and deprived of food on many occasions when he wouldn't eat what *they* wanted him to eat. Nathaniel complained that his teeth hurt him at times. Nathaniel was often told to stop his crying, or she would continue with the beatings.

Next to testify was Nathaniel who, by this time, was 11 years old.

Nathaniel, by contrast, appeared calm and controlled.Being controlled was something he had become quite conditioned to. He was, however, consistent in his testimony and in his recollection of events.

Nathaniel explained that Susan was his stepmother and Greg was his father since he was about two years old. This was about the time they moved into the Pastor's home in Scarborough.

Susan looked after home schooling and was responsible for the majority of the punishments that were meted out.

Punishments included seclusion in his room and no food.He recalled he had no food for four days when he was about seven years old. He was permitted to leave his room to use the washroom and on occasion another mother in the home would bring him food.

Nathaniel was punished in this fashion for swearing and was told by Greg that he would get food but only if he admitted that he admitted his wrongdoing.

Nathanial confirmed Ricky's testimony about having been beaten in the washroom by Susan. Nathaniel stated that he had shown the marks and bruises to Ricky.

On some occasions, Greg would just stand around and watch and wouldn't participate nor would he intervene to help Nathaniel.

He stated that he had never seen a doctor. Even though he received a blistering burn resulting from his mother spilling soup on his arm. When the Pastor was notified, she put ointment on it, and she prayed.He never saw a dentist despite reporting his teeth hurt. Again, praying was the treatment.

Nathaniel described his beatings differently – a swat or a spanking. A spanking involved pants being pulled down and hand strikes on his bare bum. It was usually Susan but not with her hand. She would use whatever she could get her hands on – with a stick or something.

He was continuously blamed for things that were neither his fault nor his doing. Despite that, his only way to escape punishment was to admit to whatever it was.

He was just being a kid.

Susan took the stand and testified in her own defence.

She told the Judge that she and Greg moved into the Pastor's home when Nathaniel was three years old. She helped with the home schooling alongside the Pastor's husband Doug and another church member.

She stated that she assumed the role of stepmother and disciplinarian. She told the court that she did spank Nathaniel and had occasionally sent him to his room. She would also give Nathaniel an extra chore to do for punishment.

She testified that she never refused him food.

Susan did admit to the Judge that she had used a wooden spoon and her hand to strike Nathaniel, using enough force to make him feel it; clarifying that she felt that she used the proper amount of force.She stated that she struck him 8-10 times at the most, always with his pants up.

Once all the witnesses had testified, the court recessed for the Judge to consider the testimony and the evidence presented to the court.

On the next appearance date in court, we were ready to hear the verdict.

COUNT 1: Assault Verdict: **NOT GUILTY**

COUNT 2: Failing to Provide the Necessities of Life verdict:

NOT GUILTY

They were free to go back to their lives with reinforced confidence that their lifestyle and beliefs were supported.

As the Judge, defence counsel and court staff dispersed back to their daily routine, I just stood there, with the crown attorney, shocked.

After hearing the testimony of an eyewitness and the testimony of Nathaniel with respect to the assault in the bathroom…. What else do you need? What does it take? What did they want to hear?

How many days of deprivation from food is acceptable?Does a child have to be reduced to skin and bones and be non-functioning to be believed?

On May 13, 1987, the preliminary inquiry took place involving the Pastor and her husband Doug. Once again, the assigned Crown Attorney was Karen Dunlop.

Despite the outcome of the preliminary inquiry for Susan and Greg, Karen and I felt confident about presenting the evidence for this inquiry.

As expected, the first witness to testify was Ricky. Ms. Dunlop spent a great amount of time with Ricky reviewing his previous testimony and interviews with the police in order to make him feel more comfortable.

Ms. Dunlop asked Ricky to elaborate on an event which occurred in August 1984.

Ricky replied, "my mother tried to, or asked me, to sleep with her" "it occurred in my room, I was in bed" "it was at night" "she woke me up …. She called to me, or she began talking as I recall."

Ricky was asked what his response was, "I was, I didn't say

much. I stuttered and I made it clear that I didn't want to....
that I didn't want to sleep with her"

Ms. Dunlop asked what his mother's response was to that.

Ricky replied, "she said that I must because I needed to be
purified and it was God's will or God's way."

Ms. Dunlop asked if his mother touched him.

Ricky replied, "she began touching me everywhere, my groin"
"my penis.... she touched it with her hand."

Ms. Dunlop asked how long his mother touched him for.He
replied, "oh I guess it was more than just a touch...I was frozen"
"she closed her hand around it and her hand moved up and
down" "she kept preaching to me that it was God's way."

Ricky's demeanor began to change dramatically when giving
evidence and explaining details about this interaction with his
mother, prompting Ms. Dunlop to ask if Ricky was okay and if
he needed a break. He wanted to continue.

Ricky went on to explain, "in as many words she said it was
God's will that she sleeps with me, and we'd be together."

Ricky stated that his mother was partially undressed, her
upper body exposed .... "ummm I was ... I was very confused.
I don't know what I was thinking then, and I was scared".

Ricky testified that his mother was standing beside his bed
while she was touching him until

"She got on top of me" "I don't .... she tried.... I couldn't"

Ms. Dunlop asked what she tried to do, Ricky replied, *I guess
she tried to put me inside her."*

The Judge asked Ricky if his mother was successful in that
attempt. Ricky replied, "no". The Judge then asked what
happened next and Ricky replied, "she cut me"

With what and where? He replied, "it was a leather... or a
razor knife rather" "she cut me on my side."

Ms. Dunlop asked why his mother had cut him. Ricky stated, "because I didn't want to sleep with her…. I had to be purified".

Ms. Dunlop asked the court about the possibility of a short break as she sensed that this was difficult testimony for Ricky. The break was granted despite the fact that Ricky wanted to press on, telling the court his story.

When court resumed, photographs of Ricky's healed injuries and the resulting scars were shown to the court. Ricky identified these photographs as his scars and the photographs were entered into evidence. Ricky also identified the red box cutter knife as belonging to his mother and as the one used to inflict his injuries. This knife was also entered into evidence.

Ms. Dunlop returned to questioning Ricky about the sexual assault in an effort to have Ricky be more specific in his descriptions.

Ricky replied, "my penis ma'am…. her vagina ma'am"

When Ricky was clarifying the acts performed and the resulting injuries sustained, his voice dropped in volume and his head hung down. This prompted the Defence Counsel to interject and state, "I can't hear the witness". This occurred many times throughout Ricky's testimony.

Ms. Dunlop inquired about another incident which occurred in August 1984.

Ricky replied, "I was …. I was being beaten and struck by Doug with a piece of driftwood" (which Ricky identified as an exhibit when presented to the court) Ricky also testified that this incident was his breaking point and he struck Doug in the face, breaking his glasses, and cutting his forehead. His mother was present during the entire event and did nothing to stop the assault nor protect Ricky.

Ms. Dunlop asked Ricky about his recollections of an event

that occurred in September 1984 at a friend's cottage.

Ricky testified when there was no one else present at the cottage, his mother approached him and stated, "she wanted to sleep together."

Once again, the defence counsel interjected that he couldn't hear the witness.

Ricky testified that after his refusal to sleep with her, she once again cut him with the knife.

As the defence counsel still could not hear Ricky's testimony, he advised the court that he and his clients needed to hear the evidence being presented and asked the court if Ricky could stand instead of remaining seated.

Ricky stated he would stand.

Ricky testified that in October 1984 he tried to escape the home and run away. He was held back by his mother's husband, Doug, along with several other members.He recalled, "they were all...what they referred to as speaking in tongue very loudly and praying for me and some were singing" "I wanted to go live with my father."

Several weeks later, when no one was home, Ricky escaped and went to live with his father "I went upstairs and took my bags which I already packed, I had a gym bag and a pack, and I climbed through my window onto the kitchen roof, and I left.I ran through the forest near my house where my father picked me up. I had called him previously."

Ricky told the court that he was taken out of school in grade 6 and that his education came from home schooling with Doug as his teacher. Ricky confirmed for the court that he never saw a doctor for any of his injuries nor a dentist for regular checkups or his complaints of toothaches. Praying was always his mother's prescription for healing.

A Dentist was called to testify. Ricky was taken to a dentist after going to live with his father. The dentist advised the court that when he first examined Ricky, he found nine cavities and needed to remove two teeth.

Defence counsel attempted to refute Ricky's claims of never being out of the house or having a normal childhood by advising the court that Ricky had been to Europe, had taken soaring (glider plane) lessons, swimming lessons, and going to a cottage. Ricky countered by stating, "I was never left alone nor was I ever unsupervised.... even on a trip to the local library"

Ricky's brother, Ron, testified and corroborated the lifestyle and discipline of the home as well as the incidents of abuse at the hands of their mother.

The Judge, after hearing and weighing all the evidence presented, determined that there were sufficient grounds to proceed to trial on all the charges against the Pastor and Doug, except for the charge of Fail to Provide the Necessities of Life.

On July 13th, 1987, the trial for the Pastor and Doug commenced at Superior Court. The Crown Attorney for this trial was Mr. John McMahon. Madame Justice Heather Smith presided.

Ricky was the first witness to testify. He appeared calmer and more relaxed that he had in previous court appearances. Sadly, he had become accustomed to talking about the abnormal circumstances of his upbringing. Despite having to verbalize all the uncomfortable details, including sexual advances made by his own mother, he presented as consistent in his testimony and very credible.

Ron testified as well. He stated that in September or October 1984, Ricky came to live with their father and him in their apartment. A few months later, he and Ricky were in the sauna and that was when he first observed marks on Ricky. They were fresh scars but not bleeding. He asked Ricky how he got those marks. Ricky refused to talk about it, and he was *"almost in tears".*

Ricky's father took the stand to testify. He advised the court that there were no scars on Ricky when he left the home eight years prior. He stated that when Ricky came to live with him, "I gave him support, schooling, the Army and freedom".

The defence counsel called a medical doctor as a witness. This doctor had been the examining physician for Ricky's application to join the Army. This examination was not in depth and the doctor stated that he had no specific notes with respect to seeing any scars during the examination, as any marks were generally overlooked.

Doug was the next to take the stand in his own defence. Doug told the court that he had a university degree and therefore taught Ricky's schooling. He recalled that in August 1984 he disciplined Ricky with a piece of driftwood for being disobedient. He struck him, "a couple of times on his rear". He stated that he did not use excessive force and Ricky just stood there. Then Ricky hit him.

Doug told the court that he never saw any scars and that no sexual assaults had occurred.

The Pastor took the stand in her own defence. She was specifically asked by the defence counsel if she had ever wounded, assaulted, or sexually assaulted her son.

She denied it all. The Pastor stood by her denials even when questioned directly by Mr. McMahon about specific incidents. She stated that because Ricky wanted to wear blue jeans that "they were unsatisfactory in Biblical terms and the Bible prohibits lust. The discipline was because he kept his room messy". She referred to the Bible as the absolute word and the last word, "If it's God's will then it must be done". She even went as far as to say that Ricky, "was out of whack and wanted to get even".

In fact, her testimony would almost have you believe that she and Ricky had been living completely different lives under the same roof.

The Pastor was asked about the day her son Ron left to go live with his father. She replied, "I escorted him down the driveway to his father and Ron's anger was directed at his father". In her mind she had done nothing wrong.

She was asked why Ron would go live with his father then, she replied, "those who are judgemental of others are like them".

After a two-day trial, and once the witnesses had completed their testimony, an opportunity was given to the defence counsel and the crown attorney to summarize the aspects of the case and give their submissions to the court.

The defence counsel made submissions first. He said that all of Ricky's testimony was a big lie and should be discounted. He told the court that Ricky's recollections were "childish fabrication" and that the scars were probably "self-inflicted". He told the court that Ricky's motive was that he had a grudge and therefore his clients should be found not guilty and the charges against them should be dismissed.

The Crown Attorney, Mr. McMahon, obviously felt differently. He pointed out that the defendants had used a tree branch for discipline and that this discipline went far beyond "a couple of times on his rear" and had occurred on more than one occasion. The Pastor was party to these offences. Mr. McMahon reminded the court that Ricky was consistent, credible, and not vindictive in his testimony. He was most certainly not "out of whack". Ricky was able to identify the objects used in the assaults and had wounds on him when he escaped the home. Ron testified to seeing the scars and he had no motive to lie. The doctor who was called by defence counsel admitted that he wasn't looking for scars as they were not an important part of the physical exam, and he therefore would not have asked any questions as to their origin.For these reasons Mr. McMahon was requesting the court find the defendants guilty on all the charges.

On July 15th, 1987, Madame Justice Heather Smith, upon reviewing all the evidence and testimony presented by both crown and defence, was ready to present her decision.

To start, she set out a timeline which included the creation of the church, schooling for Ricky, and the framework for her dictatorship and discipline, which if not followed, would incur God's wrath. Madame Justice Smith disputed Doug's version of events regarding the assault on Ricky with the driftwood stick. She believed, "Ricky is telling what happened as clearly, as accurately as possible" and "I find it was excessive by this court's standards…. Well beyond". She continued, "because there was a pause in the discipline it was clearly an assault afterwards without consent which constitutes excessive force".

Madame Justice Smith's decision rendered against Doug:

CHARGE 1: Assault with a Weapon Verdict:**GUILTY**

She deemed the Pastor a party to this offence but did register an **AQUITTAL** on that charge.

She referenced the Pastor's lack of eye contact when testifying, her lack of direct answers and her constant reference to the Bible when questioned. She stated the Pastor, "denied everything and said there were no scars".

Although she found the Pastor "a very powerful person" she

noted, "I find too many inconsistencies in the Pastor's evidence, and she is not compelling or credible".

She continued, "I do find however that Ron and his father's evidence was appreciative, candid, credible and compelling. I accept the evidence of Ron and his father's testimony".

She also disregarded the testimony of the doctor who testified for the Defence, stating "he had the paperwork filled out by a Corporal before he saw Ricky and the examination was just to determine whether he was fit or not".

With respect to Ricky's testimony regarding the sexual assaults she found, "he was forthright, responsive and direct. His voice dropped. I found him totally genuine, credible and most impressive and I accept his evidence on all of the sexual assault charges".

She also accepted the evidence of using the razor blade knife to cut Ricky during the sexual assaults. She went on to mention a statement from Ricky when he told his girlfriend, "I thought I was to blame, and I was afraid of people's reactions".

Madame Justice Smith found the Pastor **GUILTY** on the following charges:

Sexual Assault x 2, Aggravated Assault x 2, Counselling to Commit an Indictable Offence x 2, and Weapons Dangerous x 1.

All these offences occurred two years prior to Ricky's disclosure about his life with his mother the "Pastor". To obtain a conviction on offences which occurred so far in the past was elating.

On September 9th, 1987, Madame Justice Smith sentenced the Pastor to four months in custody. She served the full sentence in a Provincial Correctional Facility. Her husband, Doug, was placed on Probation.

Did their punishments fit their crimes?

13

Chapter 13

NATHANIEL'S LIFE POST TRIAL

Nathaniel died in the arms of his wife on March 24th, 2019, at the age of 44.

The official cause of his death was pneumonia. As the investigator who became intimately involved in his childhood and saved him from his personal Hell on earth, I was not really convinced that was all that caused his death.

According to a woman who had been Nathaniel's close friend since they were in elementary school, he was "different" right off the bat. She advised that they were about 12 or 13 years old when they met, and they became instant friends.

Over the years of knowing Nathaniel, she advised that he was never truly happy. He had difficulty trusting anyone in the outside world, especially women due to his two failed marriages. However, his children were very important to him.

She described his love of heavy metal music, his penchant for getting into a lot of fights (on one occasion fighting 6 guys) and his involvement with gangs. His PTSD and anger issues fueled many of his altercations. She described one such occasion where someone ran her off the road and Nathaniel, in turn, ran that person off the road. She advised that Nathaniel had many tattoos and numerous cigarette burns on his body.

Whenever the topic of sexual assault came up, he didn't offer much information, but she didn't press the point, instead advising him that she was always there to support and listen to him.

The two of them remained as close as brother and sister until Nathaniel died.

His widow remains one of the other few sources to help us understand Nathaniel and she desperately wanted to reveal the rest of his story. She is a Personal Support Worker who lives north of Toronto and gave birth to Nathaniel's son in 2012. He had previously fathered five other children with several women although those relationships never seemed to last.

His biological mother was Aboriginal, and his father was from the Caribbean Island of Trinidad. Nathaniel's obituary photo was representative of the life he led. For the most part it was a life that did not bring him joy.However, his final few years were his happiest.

She advised that the Children's Aid Society removed Nathaniel from his mother's care when he was just an infant. The couple who adopted him, Susan, and Greg, would become intimately involved in the cult.

After being removed from their custody, Nathaniel was a traveller though the foster care system. He was eventually placed in a loving foster home when he was fourteen years old. He was restless and left when he reached the age of eighteen, when he could decide in own path in life.

However, even as an adult, he sought solace and comfort

with this particular foster father who became special to him. Nathaniel bonded well with him and relied on him for advice and guidance and a place to stay whenever his life was in turmoil.

Before his death, Nathaniel had talked to his wife about his life and wished he could write a book about it. "I think it may have been fate that brought you to find me, David, to complete his wishes", she said.

His wife told us "We met in a Tim Horton's coffee shop in 2014 and it was love at first sight. I knew his health was bad, and he had several heart attacks while we were married including one time where I found him collapsed on the floor and gave him CPR. He would have died if I didn't know what to do. He eventually had a pacemaker installed.

And his teeth were very bad. I think this went back to his time living with his adoptive parents when he was a young child and they refused him any dental care at all. Although his adopted parents lived separately from the Pastor, they spent a lot of time with her and always seemed to take Nathaniel to her home when he needed disciplining.

His adopted mother Susan regularly beat him with a stick and or a wooden spoon at the urging of the Pastor and he grew to hate his adopted mother to the point where he wanted to kill her. And he was just a young kid!"

Nathaniel worked as a welder until, at age 31, he had to quit because of his ongoing heart condition. The rest of his life was spent living on a government-sponsored disability program.

Nathaniel was not one to just sit around and joined several motorcycle gangs.

"He was not perfect and served time in jail while he was in the gangs" his wife remembered. "It's nearly impossible to get out of a gang without being badly beaten or killed by other members. But Nathaniel managed it another, painful way.

There was a fight between two members, and one had pulled a gun on the other member to put an end to it. Nathaniel stepped in the way and stopped the murder. But the shooter later tried to kill Nathaniel with a crowbar to his head. He survived and the gang let him leave with his honour intact."

He sometimes spoke to his wife about his childhood that had left him psychologically and physically scarred for life.

"He spoke about being sexually abused by another member of the cult but could not bring himself to elaborate. And the Pastor used to torture Nathaniel by putting an elastic band tightly around his penis and scrotum to punish him for some misdeed. He also told me about being locked in his room for several days without food.

Thanks to one of his friends, he was able to eat potato chips and chocolate bars and soft drinks he had smuggled into his room for him. But when we were together, he suffered terribly from Post Traumatic Disorder, and he would sleepwalk four or five times a week.

My Nathaniel, despite his background, was a social butterfly and had a large circle of friends. Unfortunately, these friendships involved heavy beer drinking and his health never improved."

When he was apprehended from the cult home, one of the questions he asked the Children's Aid Society workers was if he would meet his biological mother. She did contact him once he was in foster care, but they never met until 2006. They became close. They remained close until she died of a heart attack in 2011. Once again, life had dealt him a bad hand.

Nathaniel's adoptive parents, Greg, and Susan, tried to

maintain contact with him and nearly every month, phoned him and said they would forgive him for everything HE had put THEM through.

As a police investigator, I tried to maintain a neutral attitude towards those I had arrested and charged, but as I spoke to Nathaniel's wife after his death, I began to feel physically sick when I realized the extent of the abuse and all the details I had not known at the time of the investigation.

On the night of Nathaniel's death, his wife finally got the release she had been seeking. Greg and Susan showed up at her house and she vented on them.

"I unloaded on them for the hell they had put Nathaniel through. But Susan denied it all and said she tried to be the best mother she could. I was angry; but after three or four hours berating them, I felt strangely peaceful".

And how did I feel about Nathaniel's death? Ultimately it was the pneumonia, however I believe that his hellish childhood, the beatings, and psychological abuse at the hands of the Pastor and his parents, led to his early death. As a child, Nathaniel lived an existence that no one should have had to endure.

The effects carried on well into his adult life.

He was just worn out and not able to fight any more.

EPILOGUE

If you speak to retired police officers, they often have that one case that will forever change them……. this was mine. The details of this case still bother me.

How could religious beliefs turn out to be the justification for such cruelty? Pastors, Priests, Rabbis and Ministers are often the first ones that troubled people reach out to for help to find some direction in their lives. The Pastor of this tiny cult, His Rest Christian Fellowship, turned out to be a monster.

It all began for me with a simple phone call and as my investigation progressed, I was overwhelmed by the lack of information that anyone in Canadian law enforcement had about cults, despite their inherent dangers. I was overwhelmed by the assistance from Ian Haworth on how cults operate, plus the statements of former members of this cult who willingly came forward.

With the help of various individuals and groups, including a concerned Toronto school guidance counsellor, Toronto and Durham Children's Aid Society workers, police colleagues from Toronto and Durham Regional Police Services, and a former cult member, who has made it his life's work to expose and eliminate cults of all kinds, this case was able to be investigated and successfully concluded.

Collectively we had saved Nathaniel's life and put an end to a monstrous cult which, if left unchecked, may have done more damage to other vulnerable members of society.

As I listened to Nathaniel's widow speak about what he had disclosed to her about his childhood, I thought how it would have been helpful to know all that information at the time of the investigation. I realized, however, that he was unable to disclose everything to us at that time.

At the time of the investigation, Nathaniel was a mere 10 years old! Since he was a baby, this had been his life. He had sadly become accustomed to it. He knew nothing else.

THIS was his normal.

You didn't eat? You were beaten. You cried? You were beaten.

You didn't follow the rules of the Pastor? You were beaten.

You caused trouble? You were locked in your room without food for days.

Sadly, this was daily life for Nathaniel.

Doesn't every kid live this way??? His friend Ricky grew up this way. So, it must be okay right??? Where do people get this idea that they can somehow use religion as a crutch to better themselves in life by creating a living Hell for every life they touch?

I can speak for myself and all the people in society that do not follow these 'religious cults' in saying that I do not fault Nathaniel, 10-year-old child, who bravely took the witness stand and testified that his life was, "Ahh, no big deal" just a normal kid growing up".

That was his reality. This was his normal.

However, throughout his whole adult life, that child never forgot the pain he had endured. It's no surprise that he got into serious trouble, ran with a motorcycle club, had tattoos covering most of his body, had nightmares, and sleepwalked. All the while his 'so-called parents' only thought of themselves and 'granted forgiveness' for the pain and suffering HE put THEM through!

I find comfort in believing that Nathaniel is now at peace and is reunited with his biological mother.

Ricky currently lives out of the province and keeps in touch from time to time with his brother, Ron. I contacted Ron for the purposes of this book and, although he was grateful for all that Lynn Factor and I had done for his family, he declined to be interviewed, wishing to leave that part of his life behind.

This case is just one example of how child abuse occurred behind closed doors in front of adults who should have stepped forward to report the abuse and neglect.

As an odd mathematical coincidence, Ricky's first interview was June 9th, the Search Warrant was July 9[th,] and the sentencing date was September 9th....... 999.... when flipped....666......?

A sign perhaps?

As I sit here on Father's Day finishing this book, I wish Nathaniel a "Happy Father's Day."

About the Author

In 2008, after 30 years of service, Detective David Carter retired from the Toronto Police Service. He is an accredited Domestic Violence Investigator, Sexual Assault/Child Abuse Investigator and Suspicious Death Investigator. He spent the majority of his career in the Detective field, which encompasses these areas and many more.

He was successful in obtaining many convictions for sexual assault. He received a thank you letter from a Crown Attorney for his tenacity in a difficult case involving a three-year-old sexual assault victim who testified. The other witnesses in that case were four boys ages seven and nine.

For his dedicated work in this cult investigation, David was awarded "Police Officer of the Month" for November 1987 from the Toronto Junior Board of Trade/Toronto Jaycees.

In May 1989, at the Ontario Police College in Aylmer Ontario, David was a featured presenter at the Special Conference for the Institute for the Prevention of Child Abuse. David presented this investigation before an audience of police officers, lawyers, and Children's Aid Society members.

A successful career is knowing and believing that you somehow made a difference.Although David appreciated formal recognition from his peers for a job well done, the thank-you letters, cards, and occasional baking he received from families he helped during his career touch his heart the most.

David was able to make an impact in many victims lives and not just from an investigative standpoint. A previous victim, that David had remained close to, even asked him to stand in for her father at her wedding. Imagine making that much of an impact in someone's life.

In his retirement, David enjoys camping and spending time with his family and grandchildren.

You can connect with me on:

🐦 https://twitter.com/inmymothershome

Manufactured by Amazon.ca
Bolton, ON